Beyond Absurdity

Also by Victor L. Cahn:

The Disrespectful Dictionary

Beyond Absurdity

The Plays of Tom Stoppard

Victor L. Cahn

Rutherford • Madison • Teaneck
Fairleigh Dickinson University Press
London: Associated University Presses

Associated University Presses, Inc.
Cranbury, New Jersey 08512

Associated University Presses
Magdalen House
136–148 Tooley Street
London SE1 2TT, England

Library of Congress Cataloging in Publication Data

Cahn, Victor L
  Beyond Absurdity.

  Bibliography: p.
  Includes index.
  1. Stoppard, Tom—Criticism and interpretation.
I. Title.
PR6069.T6Z6   822'.9'14   78–64920
ISBN 0–8386–2366–2

PRINTED IN THE UNITED STATES OF AMERICA

to my mother,

Evelyn Baum Cahn,

with whom I share so much,
including a love of theater,
and to whom I owe so much more

Contents

Acknowledgments

I wish to thank the following persons for their assistance:

Professor Gerald P. Lahey, for his counsel and encouragement during the initial stages of this book.

Professor George Winchester Stone, Jr., for his many kindnesses and invaluable scholarly guidance, without which this book would never have been completed.

My brother, Dr. Steven M. Cahn, for his contributions, intellectual and otherwise, that are beyond expression in mere words.

I wish to thank the following publishers for having given me permission to quote from published works:

Grove Press, Inc., for permission to quote from Tom Stoppard, *Rosencrantz and Guildenstern Are Dead*, copyright (c) 1967. Also for permission to quote Tom Stoppard, *Travesties*, copyright (c) 1975. Reprinted by permission of Grove Press, Inc.

Faber and Faber Limited, for permission to quote from Tom Stoppard, *Rosencrantz and Guildenstern Are Dead*, 1967, and *Travesties*, 1975.

Introduction

Every time is in need, but each time experiences its need in a way peculiar to itself.[1]

Poetry always expresses the basis of feeling (or sensibility) of the age in which it was written.[2]

Ours is an age of uncertainty: ethical uncertainty, economic uncertainty, political uncertainty, and religious uncertainty. Previous centuries endured the breakdown of the supernatural order and the established hierarchical society, leaving each individual free to face existence without the restrictions imposed by traditional beliefs, but without the security that these beliefs fostered. Man became an independent, yet isolated, agent.

In the nineteenth century, Darwin's findings seemed to tear man away from his divine origins, leaving him a mere animal, coldly battling for survival in a world where morality and justice seemed dominated by brute force. At times societal forces appeared even more malevolent than those of a jungle. Marx depicted a world of economic warfare, where the poor were thrust by historical inevitability into a death struggle against the wealthy. And Freud set man at the mercy of biological forces, as a pathetic victim of drives within him that shaped his character and personality regardless of his will.

In this century man has had to come to grips with the concept of world war—of murder and destruction conducted on such a terrifying scale as would have seemed inconceivable just a few decades before. Suddenly man has the power to annihilate his own species and obliterate his planet. Visions of Armageddon dance before him.

Man's hope for protection against his own creations rests in government and industry, but these are now so distant and hopelessly entangled in bureaucracy that the individual feels helpless before the impersonal and overwhelming processes that rule one.

In short, life has seldom seemed so precarious and man so impotent before powers beyond his will and ken.

The Theater of the Absurd is part of the aesthetic response to such a predicament. It is an expression of man's tenuous relationship to the universe, and its influence has been worldwide.

Tom Stoppard has been called "one of the most dazzling wits and surprising minds ever to turn up in the history of the British Theater,"[3] and "the best playwright around today, the only writer. . .capable of making the theater a truly formidable and civilized experience again."[4] When he began his writing career in the 1960s, the Theater of the Absurd was at its pinnacle,[5] and Stoppard has explained the influence of that movement on his plays:

> It seemed clear to us, that is to say the people who began writing about the same time that I did, about 1960, that you could do a lot more in the theater than had been previously demonstrated. "Waiting for Godot"—there's just no telling what sort of effect it had on our society, who wrote because of it, or wrote in a different way because of it. But it really redefined the minima of theatrical experience. Up to then you had to have X: suddenly you had X minus one.[6]

This book, then, has two goals. The first is to analyze in detail the texts of Stoppard's plays, observing his development from semirealistic beginnings, through his absurdist phase, and into his most recent works, which combine both traditions in an original theatrical form. The second goal is to place Stoppard's plays within the context of twentieth-century drama, as exemplars of the postabsurdist movement that theater must undergo if it is to grow out of the highly moving and stimulating, but ultimately nihilistic, tradition of "absurdity."

Beyond Absurdity

1/The Theater of the Absurd

The term "Theater of the Absurd" has been disparaged in some quarters as but a convenient critical peg upon which to place such disparate playwrights as Beckett, Ionesco, Pinter, Genet, and Arrabal. To be sure, these writers have not formalized a common doctrine of principles nor even expressed any artistic accord. Nevertheless, the classification has validity.

A full-scale discussion of the history and nature of absurd theater would be inappropriate here, for that task has been effectively completed in Martin Esslin's pioneering work *The Theatre of the Absurd.*[1] Additional valuable analysis may be found in John Killinger's *World in Collapse: The Vision of Absurd Drama.*[2] But for the purposes of this study of the works of Tom Stoppard, certain fundamental principles about theatrical absurdity must be established and certain fundamental questions resolved.

Essentially, absurd theater accepts the absence of a guiding symmetry in the world. God does not exist, nor does any world order normally accepted as a result of his presence. Consequently, it is said, our existence is reduced to a meaningless morass of confusion.

The reader may well ask how this vision of "absurdity" differs from the philosophical "absurdity" set forth by such writers as Camus and Sartre. There are crucial points of variance.

First, in the works of Sartre and Camus, man is clearly trapped in such an absurd world. But he is viewed as what might be called a "tragic-heroic" figure, struggling nobly against an unknowable universe, seeking to inject meaning into his life and thereby to achieve a measure of triumph over the absurdity surrounding him.

In absurd theater, however, the view of man offered might best be called "comic-pathetic." Here man is seen as little more than a clown, bumbling and fumbling his way through the incomprehensible maze that is existence, to both the amusement and the pity of the artist-observer and the audience.

A further distinction can be drawn. The viewpoint here designated "tragic-heroic' is more properly known as "existentialist," and it is essentially one of philosophical origin. The most notable contemporary names in this branch of thought are Sartre, Camus, Heidegger, and Jaspers, and, from previous generations, Kierkegaard and Nietzsche. This division of absurdity is concerned primarily with explication and debate. Albeit many existentialists write fiction and drama, at the heart of their output is philosophical argument and the reasoned promulgation of their world vision. As Thomas Bishop has written about the plays of Sartre:

> Sartre's merit lies in his ability to adapt his esoteric ideas to the requirements of the stage. . .A pioneer in a virgin field, Sartre has set high standards for those in the future who would wish to propagandize a philosophy in the theater.[3]

Such intent is precisely opposite the strategy of the playwrights of the absurd. In other words, although the plays of Sartre are clearly of considerable interest, and despite the fact that they are concerned with various aspects of the absurd, they should not be classified as part of the "theater of the absurd" tradition.

In purely theatrical terms, the plays of existentialist writers, along with the works of Anouilh, Giraudoux, de Beauvoir, and others of the group which Eric Bentley termed the "theater of the Resistance," are basically traditional. The existentialist doctrine may be philosophically revolutionary, but the fundamentals of dramatic construction, the settings, the plots, the characterizations, and the dialogue—these are firmly rooted in theatrical convention.

Such plays are *about* absurdity. They are not absurd. Esslin points out the crucial difference:

> These writers differ from the dramatists of the Absurd in an important respect: they present their sense of the irrationality of the human condition in the form of highly lucid and logically constructed reasoning, while the Theatre of the Absurd strives to express its sense of the senselessness of the human condition and the inadequacy of the rational approach by the open abandonment of rational devices and discursive thought.
>
> . . .The Theatre of the Absurd has renounced arguing *about* the absurdity of the human condition; it merely *presents* it in being—that is, in terms of concrete stage images. . . .
>
> It is this striving for an integration between the subject-matter and the form in which it is expressed that separates the Theatre of the Absurd from the Existentialist theatre.[4]

It should be added that theater has become the primary vehicle for the expression of the "comic-pathetic" division of absurdity. Beckett, Genet, Ionesco, Pinter, and others have written important fiction and poetry, but their theatrical output has dramatized the concept of absurdity with remarkable impact and to international acclaim.

In accepting the absence of order and the existence of absurdity, what intellectual consequences need be dramatized? The first is the isolation of each man. Human relationships are at best fragile commodities in the theater of the absurd. Little love and little comfort are to be drawn from the fact that each man has time and life to share with others. Characters find themselves thrown together, and they remain so not from a desire to maintain that relationship but rather from a fear of being alone.

Examples of such relationships are plentiful. Reflect upon Vladimir and Estragon in *Waiting for Godot* (1952) or Amédée and Madeleine in Ionesco's *Amédée* (1954). This latter pair suggests a corollary to man's isolation: the breakdown of family unity. This theme is presented most strikingly in Pinter's *The Homecoming* (1965), where those who survive, Ruth and Lenny, are the ones who least need love and affection.

Furthermore, when emotional love is nonexistent, physical love becomes no more than a biological urge to be satisfied. In Beckett's plays his decrepit figures are virtually asexual. Ionesco's characters are so trapped in linguistic and circumstantial quandaries that they have little time for either sex or love. In those plays where sexuality is a force, as in the works of Genet or Arrabal, it is often ugly and destructive, intensifying the loneliness each character inhabits.

With the collapse of love and human relationships and the absence of a divinity and therefore of divine justice, moral order breaks down. Values of right and wrong disappear. Horrors may pass unnoticed as characters drown themselves in the pathetic day-to-day sequence of their lives. In Ionesco's *The Killer* (1958) an entire town population is content to stand by impassively as they are systematically eliminated by a mysterious assassin. In Pinter's *The Birthday Party* (1958) members of the boardinghouse sit idly by as Stanley is menaced by McCann and Goldberg.

Thus absurd theater presents a world without divine order, without relationships, without sexual fulfillment or genuine love, and without moral awareness. Such a life is hardly precious, and consequently death holds no terror. What frightens Vladimir and Estragon about hanging themselves from the tree is not that they will both die but that only one might die, leaving one alone to live. Survival is the punishment.

Human life is not sacred, and the world is insensible to death. In Ionesco's *Exit the King* (1962), death for King Berenger I—at once an Everyman and all men—is neither heroic nor noble, but merely a pathetic loss of human power and a fade-out to nothingness. All that has come before, the triumphs of creation, the spirit of life—these are nothing in the face of extinction. The overwhelming knowledge of impending death reduces all to rubble.

Thus the transience of human life, its fragility, and its hopelessness, all must be acknowledged. In such recognition is the possibility of salvaging happiness.

These are the intellectual assumptions underlying the theater of the absurd. However, as indicated, that theater is not a propagandistic one. These values must be transformed into theatrical form, and therefore the qualities of the *theater* of absurdist drama must be considered.

William Barrett has written, "The technique of presenting the meaningless. . .consists in letting the universal disintegrate into random particulars."[5] This strategy is basic to absurd theater, for inherent in the absurdist consciousness is the chaos of life, the lack of order, symmetry, and purpose, which is properly expressed through a dramatic structure also devoid of order, symmetry, and purpose. Therefore first, an absurd play almost always consists of a series of free-floating images. Life does not have a beginning, middle, and end; neither does an absurd play. Life does not progress rationally from step to step and culminate in a dramatic climax; neither does an absurd play. In short, the dramatic conventions that have marked absurd theater have served primarily to shatter the traditional conventions of four walls; sequential plot, dialogue, action, and thought; and realistic characters and settings.

Second, playwrights of the absurd generally offer absurdity in some concrete form, often by focusing the action of their dramas on a few objects, whose incomprehensibility and intractability prove overwhelming to the characters. These objects are a manifestation of a world which seems to run riot, beyond the control of man. One thinks of the pinball machine in Adamov's *Ping Pong* (1955), which assumes deistic proportions. Or Pinter's *The Dumbwaiter* (1960), in which the title piece is transformed into a sacrificial altar, a means of submission to a divinity that chooses not to appear.

A third characteristic of absurd theater is the futility of speech, the inability of man to communicate with others and his failure to understand such plight and its consequences. Perhaps the paradigm of useless speech is to be found in Ionesco's *The Bald Soprano* (1950), which dramatizes the banalities that form everyday language—words and phrases that mean nothing and, indeed, block communication. Man flatters himself that language is a force for order. Actually it only adds to the chaos. Furthermore, when speech is useless and communication impossible, the loneliness of the individual is increased. The world is cluttered with words, yet each man is imprisoned within his own thoughts.

Language assumes more insidious dimensions in the plays of Peter Handke, specifically *Kaspar* (1967), in which language is not so much a reflection of human being as a determining force shaping that being. Kaspar is both the product and the victim of the teaching process. He is trained by society but finds himself trapped by the indoctrination he has received. His processes of thought are limited by the extent of his language.

Language in the theater of the absurd is not a cohesive force, a bond linking civilized man. Rather it is the ultimate entropistic force, isolating each man in a vacuum of words. Man is a prisoner of his own inability to communicate and of society's inability to communicate with him.

Such are the elements common to the theater of the absurd, and they have contributed to some remarkable creations. However, since the publication of Esslin's book nearly fifteen years ago, when the movement was at its height, theatrical absurdity seems to have run its course. Because the majority of absurd plays present such a hopelessly negative image, they tend to culminate in an intellectual dead end. *The Bald Soprano* concludes as the characters babble nonsense, then begin their story over again in an infinite cycle of futility. *Waiting for Godot* ends in a tableau of frozen inaction. Numerous plays end in individual death or catastrophic destruction that serves as a release from the agony of life.

Of course, many of these plays involve concepts and techniques worthy of the considerable critical attention afforded them. But one can affirm Nothing for just so long. As Arnold P. Hinchliffe has written, "The theater of Nothing, if it is to develop at all, will have to move to Something—whether the conventions and subjects are artistic, political, social or religious."[6]

It is useful to keep that thought in mind in turning to the writings of Tom Stoppard. For in just those four areas does he work and develop.

2/Stoppard the Man and His Early Full-Length Plays

Tom Stoppard was born on July 3, 1937, in Zlin, Czechoslavakia.[1] His father, Eugene Strausler, who was a company doctor with Bata, an international shoe firm, was transferred to a branch in Singapore in 1939. In 1942, when the Japanese were about to take over that naval base from the British, Tom, his mother, and his older brother moved to India. His father later died in a Japanese prison camp. After his mother married Kenneth Stoppard, an Englishman in the British army, Tom took his stepfather's name.

When the family moved to England after the war, Tom attended the Dolphin School in Nottinghamshire and the Pocklington School in Yorkshire. That was the extent of his formal education. How ironic that a writer whom such critics as Robert Brustein have labeled a mere "university wit"[2] and whose work is characterized by such philosophical erudition should never even have attended a university!

Stoppard has indicated that at seventeen he was far more interested in life than in literature,[3] and so he became a reporter, first on the *Western Daily Press* in Bristol. After four years he moved to the *Bristol Evening World*, now defunct. Starting on the police beat, he was eventually assigned to review films and plays, and he soon turned toward his own writing. In 1962 he moved to London to join *Scene Magazine* as drama critic during its nine months' existence.

Stoppard's first completed work was a stage play entitled *A Walk on the Water*, which was presented on television in 1963, a few days after President Kennedy's assassination.

Its first stage production took place in 1964 in Hamburg, Germany, during Stoppard's visit to Berlin on a Ford Foundation grant. During that five-month stay he wrote a one-act burlesque which he called "Rosencrantz and Guildenstern." The manuscript subsequently underwent many alterations, finally reaching production under the title *Rosencrantz and Guildenstern Are Dead* at the Edinburgh Festival in 1966. A year later it was performed by the National Theater to extraordinary acclaim.

In 1968 *Enter a Free Man*, the revised version of *A Walk on the Water*, was produced on stage in London, joined later that year by *The Real Inspector Hound*. Since then Stoppard has written two full-length plays, *Jumpers* and *Travesties*, in addition to several one-act, television, and radio plays, a novel entitled *Lord Malquist and Mr. Moon*, and three short stories.

Enter a Free Man (1964)

Enter a Free Man, though Stoppard's first play, was his second produced in London. Stoppard remembers that at its premiere in Hamburg it was "applauded downstairs and booed upstairs,"[4] for he had been advertised as one of the young English writers still under the influence of John Osborne and therefore still "angry."[5] But *Enter a Free Man* is in many ways a conventional domestic comedy, and a young audience expecting to hear vituperative exchanges between rebel and establishment was disappointed.

Enter a Free Man is not a startling or original piece of theater. Critics who have come across this work only after enthusiastically greeting *Rosencrantz and Guildenstern Are Dead* have noted with varying reactions the similarity of this play to Arthur Miller's *Death of a Salesman* (1949) and Robert Bolt's *Flowering Cherry* (1958). Some reviewers, like Charles Marowitz, have expressed grave disappointment.[6] Others, like Brendan Gill, have viewed the work as an interesting discovery to be considered in the light of Stoppard's recent achievements.[7]

Stoppard himself has informally referred to the play as "Flowering Death of a Cherry Salesman,"[8] frankly acknowledging the influence of the earlier works. But it would be an error to regard this first play as simply imitative. Of course, the plot, or, more properly, the situation, is familiar. George Riley is a dreamer. He imagines himself an inventor, although all his projects have failed. His long-suffering wife dutifully keeps house and shields him from the world's buffetings. His daughter, young and impatient, earns enough money to support him but remains frustrated by the narrowness of her existence and by her father's unwillingness to accept unemployment compensation. He naturally refuses such welfare on the grounds that, after all, he *is* employed. He is an inventor.

The similarities between this play and those of Miller and Bolt are obvious. The title character in each lives in a world of illusion. His wife supports his dreams, his child tries to shock him back to reality. The world outside tolerates his reveries temporarily but eventually forces him to confront the truth about himself.

However, far more important than these surface parallels are the subtle variations in character, structure, tone, and theme that distinguish Stoppard's play from the other two and from other realistic plays. At the beginning of *Death of a Salesman*, for instance, as Willy Loman drags himself into his house, he is an object of sympathy, a working man of unexceptional talent worn by age and overwork. By the end of the play he is revealed as a wreck of a man, devoid of dignity, devoted to empty dreams and hollow ideals. The play is largely humorless and as much a condemnation of the social system that fosters such delusions as a condemnation of Willy and his values. Willy has always believed in a quick smile and a pat on the back, and that a few casual friendships are substitutes for ability and work. "Be liked and you will never want."[9]

James Cherry, in *Flowering Cherry*, is also a pursuer of dreams. But whereas Willy Loman imagines himself to hold the secret of establishment success, Cherry believes he is a rebel of sorts, an individualist who is at heart an opponent of the system—here epitomized by an insurance job which, Cherry insists, stifles him.

"That's what this lousy life does for a man. It rots you. It's artificial,"[10] Cherry says. He imagines that he was meant for bigger things:

> And allow me to tell you, old man, that fifteen acres of apple trees in blossom, with a few white hens on the grass, perhaps, and some high white clouds in a blue sky, like you get in May and early June down there; it's a sight for the gods, it's Shangri-la.[11]

But at the climactic moment of the play, when his wife offers to sell the house and finance that orchard, he backs down, preferring to maintain the security of his insurance job. His grand schemes are no more than bluster.

Both Willy and Cherry are disagreeable figures. Although they bear a surface charm and are not in any way evil, their self-deception turns them ugly, and whatever good feeling they initially earn from the audience eventually disappears. They are finally beaten men who have not even put up a noble struggle. The world gets the best of them.

Not so with George Riley. His illusions may be the most hopeless of all, yet he carries them off with panache. "Enter a free man!"[12] he proclaims on his first appearance. He carries a sense of the theatrical in his life. His language, for instance, is of particular interest. His is not the typical pedestrian dialogue of the common man, but rather it has a certain grandeur.

Early in the play George dictates a letter for a young sailor friend:

> Dear Silvana, please try to forget me. I have just met a man in a pub whose example stands as a warning against even the most casual relationship with young women. A thing like that could end in disaster—twenty-five years of dead domesticity, fatal to a man of creative spirit—only today, after much loss of time and dignity. . .[P. 12]

His view of his own profession inspires the rhetorical flourish of a confidence man who has "conned" himself:

> How can I help being excited! For centuries while the balance of nature has kept flower gardens thriving with alternate sun and rain in the proportions that flowers understand, indoor plants have withered and died on a million cream-painted window-sills, attended by haphazard housewives bearing arbitrary jugs of water. For centuries. Until one day, a man noticing the tobacco-coloured leaves of a dessicated cyclamen, said to himself, what the world needs is indoor rain. [P. 36]

George lives with a style that lifts him above the realm of Willy Loman and James Cherry. They are bogged down in their existence. He seems to surmount it.

Yet whereas the audience only gradually discovers the failures of Willy and Cherry, George's plans are so whimsical and so doomed to fail that the audience can only gaze and laugh. The invention that he reveals early in the play, and that is the basis of all his hopes, is so quixotic and pathetic as to remove all suspense that might possibly inject tension in the play. He pulls out an envelope, then explains that the edges of the flap are gummed on both sides. Even when Harry, his bar-stool acquaintance, expresses enthusiasm for the project, offering to help with marketing and promotion, there is no doubt that the plan is doomed from the start.

Thus throughout the rest of the play the audience is waiting for the inevitable, waiting for that illusion to be punctured. George's dream is, therefore, an intriguing version of the tragic flaw, a "comic-tragic flaw," so to speak. Such perspective gives the play an almost classic structure, for despite the fact that the unities of time and place are not strictly observed, what still emerges is a dramatic composition of ironic force and direction.

However, an additional irony dominates the play. Because much of the play is comic, the audience expects the type of ending appropriate to a comedy, where conflicts are resolved in favor of the hero. But in the final scene in the pub, as Harry demonstrates the obvious futility of the invention, our disappointment is doubly painful. We knew that the invention was hopeless, and that in life George would have no chance of selling it. But somehow we had hoped that in a comedy the inevitable might be avoided. Our illusions collapse with George's.

Two further considerations in analyzing this play are its relationship to the theater of the absurd and how it stands as a prelude to the rest of Stoppard's work. Definite links can be drawn, links which further distinguish *Enter a Free Man* from the other two plays with which it is usually classified.

For instance, in *Death of a Salesman* the business world has its symbol in the form of Howard, the son of the man who originally hired Willy and who now refuses Willy's desperate plea for a job. Howard epitomizes a society that takes no pity on its members, and the implication of the play is that some social change might help Willy and alleviate his suffering. His struggle is not against existence but against a competitive system that forces men to battle one another for survival.

In *Flowering Cherry* the outside world is personified by Gilbert Grass of the insurance business, presented as a neutral force. For Cherry's failure is personal. If he could reconcile himself to his own abilities and character, if he could face reality, he might achieve contentment. The play is a call for maturity and self-evaluation.

In *Enter a Free Man* the world is a mysterious entity, beyond the understanding of the individual man. This apprehension, clearly a suggestion of absurdity, is offered first when Harry pretends to have a plan for submitting George's envelope to the appropriate agency. Their dialogue centers about the unknowable "them" of the business world, and Harry instructs George to fight "them" on their own terms. But the specifics are never elaborated, and the audience is left with the impression that no tactics could suffice. The world outside is half-menacing, somewhat nebulous, and always impenetrable.

A clearer suggestion of such an absurdist view of the world occurs late in Act 2:

> Hong Kong. . .colours, the colour of it all. Chinese junks and palms. . .Aden! Naples! But how do I know they are really there? For all I know, it is possible, that nothing else exists, or if it does, then in some fantastic form which, by an elaborate conspiracy, has been kept secret from me.[P. 74]

He adds a moment later:

> Odd thing is . . . I sometimes think of myself as a sailor, in a way . . . with home as a little boat, anchored in the middle of a big calm sea, never going anywhere, just sitting, far from land, life, everything. [P. 75]

The dialogue hints at profound loneliness. George intuits the essential isolation of each man and the void that surrounds him, that theme pervading absurdist drama. All his illusions, fantasies, and general theatricality are a defense against the intrusion of reality, an attempt to counter the unspoken dread of the world with a private universe of his own.

Of course, such escape is not without pain. And George is aware of the difficulties, although he does not think enough to warn himself. He knows, however, that his daughter is a hopeless romantic, who dreams of riding off into the sunset with her motorcycle friend. But at the end of the play she, too, is broken, for the cyclist deserts her. George's earlier advice to his daughter might well be a guide for himself:

> Headlong. Out of your depth. You think each moment's going to last forever and then you're brought down with a bump. You

never learn. . . .

Watch where you're going. Take stock. Test the ground. Don't jump in with your eyes shut. That's the way to get hurt. [P. 43]

Yet to dream is the only resort in the world of this play.

Mrs. Riley, named Persephone by George, although her real name is Constance, also seeks escape from the world. Linda points out her manner of retreat. "You don't care about anything except tidying up the mess. "What's the *point*? What are you being tidy *for*?" (p. 68). Her accusation is fair. Persephone, bearing the same name as the mythological queen of Pluto's underworld, does virtually nothing in the play but clean and vacuum and dust. Her reason is simple:

I've kept our life tidy—I've looked after you and him, and got you this far—perhaps it is a waste of time. You never went to sleep on a damp sheet and you never went to school without a cooked breakfast—and what was the point of that? [P. 68]

The question might be extended to mean "What is the point of anything?" It is certainly not a stretch of the text to see that Mrs. Riley perceives the world as a frightening place and that one must keep occupied to pass the time. She sees no greater glory, no afterlife, not much to this life. She will finally come to grips with the prospect that there is no "point" to anything. Thus her preoccupation with cleaning. Like Estragon and Vladimir, like Rosencrantz and Guildenstern, like a whole generation of absurdist characters, she seeks an activity which will fill up her life. Cleaning is as worthwhile as any other.

She, too, feels the essential loneliness of life. When Linda blurts out, "We're lumbered, and we'll go on being lumbered till he's dead, and that may be *years*—" (p.67), Persephone makes clear the need for unity:

But he's ours and we're his, and don't you ever talk about him like that again. (*Spent*). You can call him the family joke, but it's our family. [Pp. 67–68]

She recognizes that in such a world it is better to be in company than alone. Hence the appropriateness of her real name, Constance. Relationships may be painful at times, but the comfort of the bond is all-important. Again, this is much the attitude of characters throughout absurdist theater, for, as indicated previously, absurdist drama relationships are often awkward, but they are preferable to the terrors of loneliness.

Other bonds with absurdity may be found in this ostensibly realistic play. One of the dialogue patterns most common to absurd drama is the compilation of small sentences, each cascading upon another in a barrage of rhythm and syllables. Such a structure is utilized frequently in this play. For instance, in the first scene in the pub, Riley, Harry, and Carmen the bartender indulge in reflection on society, and their recitation is directly out of absurdity:

> HARRY: It's terrible really. I blame youth.
> CARMEN: Education.
> HARRY: The Church is out of touch.
> CARMEN: The family is not what it was.
> HARRY: It's the power of the unions.
> CARMEN: The betrayal of the navy.
> HARRY: Ban the bomb . . . [P. 15]

As it continues, it eventually degenerates into nonsense:

> HARRY: All Japanese inventors are small.
> CARMEN: They're a small people.
> HARRY: Very small. Short.
> RILEY: The little man!
> HARRY: The little people!
> RILEY: Look at the transistor!
> HARRY: Very small!
> RILEY: Japanese!
> CARMEN: Gurkhas are short.
> HARRY: But exceedingly brave for their size.
> CARMEN: Fearless.
> RILEY (*furiously*): What are you talking about! [P. 15]

This is a classic example of absurdist dialogue, much like passages in the plays of Beckett, Ionesco, and Pinter, where the sense of the words is lost amidst their force, as language assumes a strength and path of its own, independent of thought processes.

Stoppard's special contribution to absurdist language appears sporadically in *Enter a Free Man*. He delights in linguistic trickery, double meanings, and homonymic phenomena:

> RILEY: (*calling up to Harry*): A man is born free and everywhere he
> is in chains. Who said that?
> ABLE: Houdini?
> RILEY: (*turning*): Who?
> ABLE: —dini.
> RILEY: Houdini. No. [P. 13]

Such linguistic double play will be used to a much greater extent in Stoppard's later plays.

George also indulges in a preoccupation especially prevalent in absurdist drama, a dwelling in the past. Like the title charcter in Beckett's *Krapp's Last Tape*, he is drawn irresistably toward reveries about his life:

> My life is piled up between me and the sun, as real and hopeless
> as a pile of broken furniture. Thirty years ago I was a young man
> ready to leave the ground and fly. Thirty years. . .More, perhaps
> much more than the time I have left, and when a man's past out-
> weighs his future, then he's a man standing in his own shadow. . .
> [P. 33]

Ironically, thirty years is the same interval between the two tapes Krapp plays in his den.

Riley is equally tormented by the transience of his own hopes. He agonizes over the fragility of life, a crucial aspect of absurdist consciousness, and he is desperately trying to flee from the pains of reality through escape in the past. Toward the end of the play, as Linda grows more impatient with her father's fantasies, he tries to remind her of a time when she was a child and believed in him: "In the park. We used to walk in the park, and don't deny it—*you had FAITH!*" (p. 62). But Linda cannot tolerate his memories. And she berates him for storing her childhood toys and books, pathetically trying to maintain the illusion of her youth and with that, of course, his own.

The end of the play unites many of the themes. George's invention, the two-way envelope, has been thrown away. He has become reconciled to accepting unemployment compensation. He has dropped the pretense of names in the pub. The barman whom he called "Carmen" for obvious poetic reasons insists on his real name, Victor, and the sailor whom George had grandly referred to as "Able," seaman, confesses his real name is Dick. George even admits his wife's real name. The aesthetic perfection of his fantasy world has shattered. He has, for all practical purposes, surrendered his individuality.

Yet he does enjoy a moment of triumph. Throughout the play George has alluded to a network of pipes running along the walls of his home, a system which he says will create indoor rain. Linda has continually scorned the idea, but suddenly thunder is heard, water begins to drop over his plants, and he shouts in triumph. Linda, however, points out "the flaw in the ointment" (p. 84). How to turn the water off?

Linda looks at him and takes out some coins, his weekly allowance which she has provided for so long. She recognizes the joy he has received from this invention that has failed, and that he must be given the opportunity to continue his struggle against the world. That struggle is hopeless, but the very act of opposition brings meaning to George Riley's life.

Enter a Free Man thus serves as the thematic and the theatrical foundation of Stoppard's writing. It is primarily a realistic work, as Raymond Sokolov writes, "lying somewhere about midway between the well-made entertainment and the Beckett-like limbo of 'Rosencrantz.'"[13] Through intimations of absurdity, Stoppard creates his archetypal theatrical situation: a realistic, identifiable man confronting an absurd world and seeking refuge from it. In his next play, *Rosencrantz and Guildenstern Are Dead,* Stoppard confronts absurdity head-on and at the same time takes the initial steps toward moving beyond absurdity.

Rosencrantz and Guildenstern Are Dead (1966)

Rosencrantz and Guildenstern Are Dead, written in 1964, was Stoppard's initial success, the play that earned him a worldwide reputation and that remains his most notable work. It has been called "a dazzling, compassionate fantasy"[14] and "a most remarkable and thrilling play."[15] But it has also been criticized as a merely derivative work, whose debts to Beckett, Pirandello, and, of course, Shakespeare are far more important than any original contributions Stoppard brings. The quintessence of this critical view might be Robert Brustein's description of the play as a "theatrical parasite."[16]

But to so limit the world of *Rosencrantz and Guildenstern Are Dead* is to misunderstand the play and to fail to appreciate just what Stoppard has attempted and what he has accomplished. For *Rosencrantz and Guildenstern Are Dead* is a significant step in moving theater out of the abyss of absurdity. True, the dramatic conventions and intellectual elements that characterize what has now become traditional absurdist theater are present here as well. However, in addition this play contains characters who are themselves realistic, identifiable figures. C. J. Gianakaris takes note of this important dramatic innovation:

But now we have a new piece to consider which in part, at least, reconciles the disparities between drama anchored to personal/ social responsibility and that pledged to the stripping of hackneyed illusions underlying much of current life. . . .And though the format of the work derives unmistakably from absurdist drama, the sympathetic attention being paid men in their earthly dilemmas also comes across noticeably, mostly through a jeeringless laughter only rarely available to dark comedy.[17]

This, then, is the essential conflict of *Rosencrantz and Guildenstern Are Dead*, the conflict that is to become the crucial theme of Stoppard's writings. How is man to reconcile himself to that absurd world in which he finds himself trapped?

To understand the innovations that Stoppard has brought to absurdist writing it is useful to see *Rosencrantz and Guildenstern Are Dead* in light of the play to which it is most often compared, *Waiting for Godot.* Consider, for instance, the opening scenes of each play. Some critics, such as John Russell Taylor, have dismissed Stoppard's writing as completely imitative of Beckett's.[18] And, to be sure, the parallels are undeniable. In each play the audience observes a pair of men waiting on an open road for someone or something to relieve their loneliness and uncertainty. To escape the tedium of waiting, the men seek activities which will fill the time. They play-act. Estragon and Vladimir pretend to be Pozzo and Lucky, Rosencrantz and Guildenstern later pretend to be Hamlet. They play games. Estragon and Vladimir insult one another, Rosencrantz and Guildenstern flip coins and play games of questions. Both pairs reflect on life, death, time, and memory. They conduct dialogues in the cross-talk style of vaudevillian comedians. At times they must express their unity physically. When Estragon and Vladimir hear a strange sound, they huddle together, panicked (p. 13). In an early moment of loneliness Guildenstern reflects, "Your capacity for trust made me wonder if perhaps. . .you, alone. . .(*He turns on him suddenly, reaches out a hand.*) Touch."[19]

Further minor similarities can be enumerated. But of greater significance are the subtle differences of strategy and technique. For instance, Estragon and Vladimir are tramps, outside any society, deprived of role and stature. However, Rosencrantz and Guildenstern are very much a part of their society. Stoppard writes that "They are well dressed—hats, coats, sticks and all" (p. 11). Furthermore, each of them carries a large leather bag, symbolic of social standing. And although both pairs of characters are set in indefinite locations, Rosencrantz and Guildenstern are by Stoppard's direction Elizabethans, while Estragon and Vladimir are virtually timeless and lacking a home or native land.

These distinctions may seem negligible. But, in fact, they set the tone for the entire structure of the two plays. The lack of identity which Estragon and Vladimir must bear makes them virtually allegorical figures. Consequently, the audience is forced to maintain detachment and is unable to identify with the characters and share their plight.

But such is not the case with Rosencrantz and Guildenstern. They are clearly members of a society, living under certain social rules and traditions. The specific nature of these rules and traditions is irrelevant. What matters is that the two characters are part of a social system, not standing among the fragments outside it. No outside society exists in *Waiting for Godot*. There most certainly is a society in *Rosencrantz and Guildenstern Are Dead*.

Thus Estragon and Vladimir are denied a context, and under such circumstances Godot is an unknown factor, a suspicion rather than an expectation. Rosencrantz and Guildenstern, on the other hand, can analyze their situation in some detail:

GUIL: *(tensed up by this rambling)*: Do you remember the first thing that happened today?
ROS: *(promptly)*: I woke up, I suppose. *(Triggered.)* Oh—I've got it now—that man, a foreigner, he woke us up—
GUIL: A messenger. *(He relaxes, sits.)*
ROS: That's it—pale sky before dawn, a man standing on his saddle to bang on the shutters—shouts—What's all the row about?! Clear off!—But then he called our names. You remember that—this man woke us up. . .
It was urgent—a matter of extreme urgency, a royal summons, his very words: official business and no questions asked—lights

in the stable-yard, saddle up and off headlong and hotfoot across the land, our guides outstripped in breakneck pursuit of our duty! Fearful lest we come too late!!
Small pause
GUIL: Too late for what? [P. 19]

Contrast such comparative certainty with this passage from *Waiting for Godot.:*

ESTRAGON: What exactly did we ask him for?
VLADIMIR: Were you not there?
ESTRAGON: I can't have been listening.
VLADIMIR: Oh. . .Nothing very definite. [P. 13]

Indication here suggests that events of the past are but part of a shadowy mist and that memory is inherently inaccurate. However, the concretion of Rosencrantz's recollections brings a touch of realism to their drama. The two characters know that they were called that very day. Although they are uncertain about the purpose of their summoning, they are nevertheless moving toward a specific goal.

Indeed, the very opening of the play emphasizes this vision of the world. The coin game which occupies Rosencrantz and Guildenstern is above all a dramatic device, immediately absorbing audience attention and demanding involvement in the action on stage. More important, the coin game alerts the audience to a world of uncertain values. It is not a world of no values, such as the world of Godot. Rather, the world of Rosencrantz and Guildenstern is an inverted world, one of values that defy reason. It is not without reason; it is in direct opposition to it.

The unnerving element of this coin game is, of course, the incredible series of flips that have turned up heads some seventy times as the curtain rises. Guildenstern is moved to re-mark, "A weaker man might be moved to re-examine his faith, if in nothing else at least in the law of probability" (p. 12). And this line sets the pattern for what will become the crisis of the play: the breakdown of the laws of reason and order. The primary motivation of Rosencrantz and Guildenstern will be to understand what is happening to them and around them.

The play therefore is, in that sense, very much an intellectual battle, an attempt to grasp a world where events defy reason and occur seemingly without cause. And Rosencrantz and Guildenstern, always on the fringe of the activities, find themselves placed in circumstances without understanding either why they have been so placed or what they are then supposed to do. But it is important to remember that these circumstances are actually circumstances. Rosencrantz and Guildenstern are not trapped in some nondescript void. Theirs is essentially the predicament of the individual trapped in a world where the powers in charge carry on as though all events had purpose, but where that purpose nonetheless eludes the individual citizen.

This is a significant step in absurdist theater. The majority of plays from that tradition contain not even a semblance of order or purpose. The world simply runs riot. For instance, Beckett's characters do not function in terms of governmental operations or social responsibility. Existence itself, irrespective of personal relationships, is problem enough. In Ionesco's plays, such as *The Bald Soprano* or *Amédée,* confusion reigns supreme. The characters are not missing the pattern of their lives by just a small margin. Their existence is chaos, and resistance is hopeless.

John Simon has questioned the characterization of Rosencrantz and Guildenstern. He suggests that Estragon and Vladimir are well differentiated but that Rosencrantz and Guildenstern "tend to overlap and blur."[20] He states further that whether such a tactic is intentional or not, it underscores a dramatic deficiency.

Stoppard does, however, take pains to distinguish between Rosencrantz and Guildenstern at the opening of the play, as they flip coins. As the impossible run is taking place,

Ros betrays no surprise at all—he feels none. However, he is nice enough to feel a little embarrassed at taking so much money off his friend. Let that be his character note.

Guil is well alive to the oddity of it. He is not worried about the money, but he is worried by the implications; aware but not going to panic about it—his character note. [P. 11]

Gerald Weales elaborates further on the distinctions:

Guildenstern, like Valdimir, is the intellectual, spinning out syllogisms, setting up tests, working desperately in the hopes that logic or illogic will let him cut a path through the uncertainty that surrounds them. Rosencrantz, like Estragon, is a bit dense, slow to follow the turn of Guildenstern's mind, flat-footed in his own ruminations, as in his long speech on death, on being shut in a box, which sends his friend screaming.[21]

Nevertheless, inevitably some confusion surrounds the two characters, and this may be traced to two circumstances.

First, in *Hamlet* itself the two are virtually indistinguishable, from the rhythms of their names, to their actions, even to the number of syllables in their speeches. This phenomenon shall be considered in detail presently, but what matters for the moment is that Shakespeare's presentation of the two as somewhat sinister sycophants makes telling them apart most difficult, and Stoppard is naturally working within Shakespeare's framework.

Second, the nature of absurdist dialogue precludes speakers' being consistently distinguishable one from another. The dialogue patterns singled out in *Enter a Free Man* become much more prevalent in *Rosencrantz and Guildenstern Are Dead*. For instance:

Ros: Who was that?
Guil: Didn't you know him?
Ros: He didn't know me.
Guil: He didn't see you.
Ros: I didn't see him. [Pp. 45–46]

Or this passage:

> Ros: Took the very words out of my mouth.
> Guil: You'd be *lost* for words.
> Ros: You'd be tongue-tied.
> Guil: Like a mute in a monologue.
> Ros: Like a nightingale at a Roman feast.
> Guil: Your diction will go to pieces.
> Ros: Your lines will be cut.
> Guil: To dumbshows.
> Ros: And dramatic pauses. [P. 62]

Individuality necessarily disappears in such speech. Language itself takes charge. In *Waiting for Godot* such passages are plentiful, and even in a reading of that play one tends to lose track of personal identity.

A further consequence of the play's linguistic style explains why Rosencrantz and Guildenstern can at one moment speak with extraordinary eloquence and why at other times they are reduced to fumbling monosyllables. That their quality of speech should vary so greatly during the play seems indicative of some inadequacy on Stoppard's part.

However, most of the passages characterized by skillful use of language are those in which either Rosencrantz or Guildenstern speaks essentially a monologue, outpouring his own feelings without expectation of response. Such a speech is Guildenstern's initial series of conjectures as to why each flip of the coins turns up heads.

> List of possible explanations. One: I'm willing it. Inside where nothing shows, I am the essence of a man spinning double-headed coins, and betting against himself in private atonement for an unremembered past. . . .
> Two: Time has stopped dead, and the single experience of one coin being spun once has been repeated ninety times. . . . On the whole, doubtful. [P. 16]

He continues in a most rational vein, pondering a number of sophisticated philosophical postulates. Even the comparatively dull Rosencrantz has moments of lucid monologue:

> There must have been one, a moment, in childhood when it first
> occurred to you that you don't go on for ever. It must have been
> shattering—stamped into one's memory. And yet I can't remember
> it. It never occurred to me at all. What does one make of that? We
> must be born with an intuition of mortality. Before we know the
> world for it, before we know that there are words, out we come,
> bloodied and squalling with the knowlege that for all the compasses
> in the world, there's only one direction, and time is its only measure.
> [Pp. 71–72]

Thus Rosencrantz and Guildenstern are not incapable of
rationality, although Guildenstern tends to discourse on a
higher plane than Rosencrantz. Rather, it is when they must
communicate with one another rather than just soliloquize
to the audience that powers of speech fail them. The blending of two patterns of thought creates this kind of confusion:

> PLAYER: Why?
> GUIL: Ah. (To Ros:) Why?
> ROS: Exactly.
> GUIL: Exactly what?
> ROS: Exactly why.
> GUIL: Exactly why *what*?
> ROS: What?
> GUIL: Why?
> ROS: Why what, exactly?
> GUIL: Why is he mad?!
> ROS: *I* don't know! [P. 68]

Therefore it is fair to say that Rosencrantz and Guildenstern
vary in the quality of their language, but at the same time such
variety is dramatically proper.

In addition to Beckett, the other modern major dramatic
influence on *Rosencrantz and Guildenstern Are Dead* is Pirandello. Such influence is manifest most notably in the scenes
with the Players. To a great extent their plight is that of the
title characters, a quandary the chief Player presents in terms
theatrical rather than philosophical:

Why, we grow rusty and you catch us at the very point of decadence—by this time tomorrow we might have forgotten everything we ever knew. That's a thought, isn't it? (*He laughs generously.*) We'd be back where we started—improvising. [P. 22]

He is describing very closely the situation of Rosencrantz and Guildenstern. Their memories are almost blank, and so they improvise. As will be seen, in succeeding scenes the Pirandellian issues of art versus life and the theatrical nature of reality are developed further.

This initial encounter with the Players also reveals the intrinsic innocence of Rosencrantz and Guildenstern and helps break down the distance between the audience and the characters. The Players offer the pair the opportunity to participate in a private, uncut performance of "The Rape of the Sabine Women," with a boy of the company playing the woman's role. Guildenstern is morally outraged at this suggestion, and his sense of ethics removes him from the tradition of absurd theater, where right and wrong are often nonexistent. And Guildenstern's sensibilities further tend to remove him from the realm of absurdist figures, who absorb all immoralities with a fatalistic equanimity.

The predicament of Rosencrantz and Guildenstern assumes a new dimension with the entrance of the members of the court. John Simon has criticized this aspect of the treatment of *Hamlet,* specifically the characterization of Hamlet and Ophelia:

These major characters are, after all, supposed to be the mighty opposites between whose fell incenséd points our poor shrimps perish; if they are themselves only cardboard shadow-boxers, everything drifts away.[22]

But it is vital to an understanding of the plight of Rosencrantz and Guildenstern and to a general understanding of this play to realize that they do not have only a small role in what is actually a more significant action. There is no more significant action, only a series of complications beyond their knowledge. All action is equally lacking in purpose and significance.

This question of the relationship between *Rosencrantz and Guildenstern Are Dead* and *Hamlet* brings to light a series of important issues. First, what is the position of *Hamlet* within Stoppard's play? Certainly it loses much of its dignity and power. The initial blending of the two plays occurs at a point in Act 2, scene 2 of *Hamlet* and at the middle of Act 1 of *Rosencrantz and Guildenstern Are Dead*. In Stoppard's play Rosencrantz and Guildenstern have been tossing their coins once again, this time in front of the Player. The last flip occurs, and the Player turns without even checking the result, since the sequence of uninterrupted "heads" has left him frustrated and baffled. But the unchecked coin is suddenly revealed from under the Player's foot:

> GUIL: (*moving out*): Come on.
> ROS: I say—that was lucky.
> GUIL: (*turning*): What?
> ROS: It was tails. [P. 34]

This is a turning point in the play. Logic and order are suddenly restored with the appearance of what, for Rosencrantz and Guildenstern, and for the audience, too, is the "real world," perhaps more appropriately called "the recognizable world." It is a world of hierarchical order, of amenities, of dignity. Yet in Stoppard's play the court loses all those trappings of royalty and tragedy traditionally assigned to it. Ophelia and Hamlet, running around the stage, look like renegades from a Feydeau farce. And Stoppard's commentary is laced with ironic phrases from Act 2, scene 1 of *Hamlet* that further undercut the action:

> And with a look so piteous, he takes her by the wrist and holds her hard, then he goes to the length of his arm, and with his other hand over his brow, falls to such perusal of her face as he would draw it. . . .he raises a sigh so piteous and profound that it does seem to shatter all his bulk and end his being. [P. 35]

This passion is the first glimpse of the court of Elsinore that Rosencrantz and Guildenstern experience, and initially they freeze. Then Guildenstern reacts, shouting "Come on!" (p. 35). But the other members of the court enter before escape is possible.

The next sequence is bound to have a peculiar effect on the audience. After the initial shock of recognition which will accompany the entrance of the court, the audience will begin to laugh as it is confronted by a series of events that, although familiar, now seem strange and almost ridiculous. The reason is that these events are presented without cause and consequently without reason. No ghost has appeared, no murder has been recalled, nor has any unseemly marriage been attacked. And climaxing the laughter is the fascinated horror of Rosencrantz and Guildenstern, whose instincts tell them to run away as fast as possible. Whatever terrors uncertainty holds, they are preferable to the actual confusion of reality. Thus in Stoppard's play Shakespeare's *Hamlet* is deflated immediately, and its own absurdity is suggested. This will grow clearer as the play unfolds.

But Claudius begins to speak, and Rosencrantz and Guildenstern are prisoners. And now the second critical issue arises about the relationship between Shakespeare's play and Stoppard's: what roles do the pair play in each? In Stoppard's play the first lines of dialogue are accompanied by a burlesque confusion as the King mixes up the two. But such confusion is Shakespeare's invention. Throughout his play Stoppard exaggerates this uncertainty as part of the general deflation. At the end of this scene the Queen corrects the King, whereas this time he identifies them properly, and her error confuses everyone.

What follows the King's greeting is a succession of blank verse speeches, and their effect is intriguing. The juxtaposition of the earlier mundane prose exchanges and the convoluted poetic expressions is at first jarring, then quite funny. It is extremely difficult for the audience to adjust to the pace

of the new language, and the passages seem more like expressions of nonsense than communication. Furthermore,
when Rosencrantz and Guildenstern respond in blank verse,
their words carry a sense of mechanization, of meaningless
jargon they are forced to utter as formalistic response. In
addition, the rhythmic similarity of their speeches emphasizes
their lack of individuality:

> Ros: Both your majesties
>   Might, by the sovereign power you have of us,
>   Put your dread pleasures more into command
>   Than to entreaty.
> Guil: But we both obey,
>   And here give up ourselves in the full bent
>   To lay our service freely at your feet,
>   To be commanded. [P. 36]

They speak like puppets, incapable of thought, placed in
a dramatic situation where certain words must emanate from
them, and like parrots they imitate the rhythms they have
just heard from their superiors.

It is the reaction of Rosencrantz and Guildenstern to this
first court scene that obliterates the sense of theatrical detachment. Rosencrantz's response is "I want to go home"
(p. 37). That line could not be found in any totally absurdist
play, for the concept of home and security are alien to absurdity. Rosencrantz and Guildenstern bring themselves a new
dimension, that of figures caught in two lives: one amidst the
outside world, one within themselves. Existence therefore
assumes two levels, the absurd world surrounding and the
interior haven of one's mind and soul. Rosencrantz and Guildenstern would prefer to retreat to that latter level, but the
absurd world constantly intrudes. As Rosencrantz says: "Never
a moment's peace! In and out, on and off, they're coming
at us from all sides" (p. 73).

Their recourse is to accept events as they come and hope
to survive:

Ros: For how long?

GUIL: Till events have played themselves out. There's a logic at work—it's all done for you, don't worry. Enjoy it. Relax. To be taken in hand and led, like being a child again, even without the innocence, a child—it's like being given a prize, an extra slice of childhood when you least expect it, as a prize for being good, or compensation for never having had one. [P. 40]

One thinks immediately of Pirandello here, and therefore a brief digression into the nature of his theater would be helpful.

Pirandello's work may be said to have shattered the gap which had always existed between stage and audience, between art and life, between intellect and passion:

What is dramatic 'reality' and 'dramatic illusion?' What does it mean to 'act' on a stage? What is the relationship between the uses of the verb 'act' to denote the straightforward movements within the order of nature and sham movements, pretenses, within the order of artifice? Finally, what are the relationships between reality and truth, human characters and the characters of a fiction, imagination and actuality? [23]

Such questions have always plagued dramatists, but none has ever approached the problem so directly as Pirandello. No doubt his most famous play is *Six Characters in Search of an Author* (1921), in which the audience is confronted with two groups on stage: one, a group of traditional characters, here actors rehearsing a script; the other, a group of "characters" from within a script, seeking an author to permit them to carry out their unfinished drama. Both groups manifest conflicts. The traditional actors are demonstrating the inevitable failure of art to recreate life. How can life, which is flowing, irregular, and mutable, be recreated in art, which is fixed, regular, and immutable? The actors are perpetually trying to escape the mutability of their lives by playing a role, seeking sanctuary in the permanence of art, a secure,

eternal truth. The second conflict is manifested in the "characters." They are imprisoned in a fixed existence, playing
their one role, and struggling to experience the variability
of life.

The struggle of the individual man to resolve this conflict
is dramatized in Pirandello's other masterpiece, *Henry IV*
(1922). Here the protagonist, while twenty years before dressed
as King Henry IV of Germany for a pageant, was thrown
from his horse and lost consciousness. When he revived, he
actually believed he was the ancient king whom he had been
impersonating. Rather than have him committed to an asylum,
his family has humored him for all these years, maintaining
the world of the court around him. However, the climactic
moment of the play occurred twelve years before the present
action, when Henry awoke out of his amnesia but decided
to retain his pose of madness, to continue to live the role of
the ancient king. He saw the sordid real world and rather
than return to it, to assume a role in its frightening, uncontrol-
lable flow, he resolved to remain in the fixed world of artistic
form. For in that role of Henry IV he is free from all responsibilities. His action, his thoughts, his morality, all are laid
out for him, much like the script of a play. He is thus both
imprisoned and free at the same time: imprisoned in that
role and unable to act on his own, but free from the need
of *having* to act on his own.

The relationship of Henry IV to Guildenstern is important.
Guildenstern, too, wishes to escape into form, to be free from
the vicissitudes of life, and to take comfort in the permanence
of direction and art. Like many other Stoppard characters
to be considered, he wants to escape having to plan and think
and wonder. Then he might enjoy the freedom of not being
free, relief from the burden of autonomy.

But circumstances force him and Rosencrantz to continue
their search for meaning, and they begin their inquiry into
the nature of Hamlet and his so-called "transformation,"
that antic behavior which occupies so much of the court's

time in both *Hamlet* and *Rosencrantz and Guildenstern Are Dead*. This question of meaning is the third critical issue centering on the relationship of Stoppard's play to Shakespeare's. Rosencrantz and Guildenstern approach the problem by repeating the words of Gertrude and Claudius, who had urged them to "glean, whether aught to us unknown afflicts him thus. . ." (p. 36) They say such lines over and over, seeking hidden meaning:

> GUIL: *Retentive*—he's a very retentive king, a royal retainer. . .
> Ros: What are you playing at?
> GUIL: Words, words. They're all we have to go on. [P. 41]

And Rosencrantz adds, standing at the footlights:

> How very intriguing! (*Turns.*) I feel like a spectator—an appalling business. The only thing that makes it bearable is the irrational belief that somebody interesting will come on in a minute. [P. 41]

In other words, the two are but spectators at a performance of *Hamlet*, given no information and expected somehow to discern the secret of Hamlet's character and the significance of his actions. The task is precisely one that has occupied Western man for the past few centuries. Provided with only the text of *Hamlet*, critics have written hundreds of volumes in an attempt to grasp the essence of the play. The bibliography continues to grow, and the humorous cross-talk of Rosencrantz and Guildenstern, filled with tentative suggestions and theories, is in fact a compressed, if comically confused, portrait of literary criticism. They conclude as follows:

> Ros: To sum up: your father, whom you love, dies, you are his heir, you come back to find that hardly was the corpse cold before his young brother popped onto his throne and into his sheets, thereby offending both legal and natural practice. Now why exactly are you behaving in this extraordinary manner?
> GUIL: I can't imagine! [Pp. 50–51]

It is an effective reduction of the plot of *Hamlet*, made even more effective by the overtones of the parody of critical inquiry.

With the entrance of Hamlet at the end of Act 1 and the beginning of his conversation with Rosencrantz and Guildenstern, the three critical issues listed above become inextricably tied together. For during the second act of Stoppard's play the characters and lines of *Hamlet* are interspersed at a much more frequent pace, and the overriding question becomes how much of Stoppard's play is found in Shakespeare's and how much and to what end does Stoppard rework Shakespeare's play. As preparation for this discussion it is useful to consider once again that first court scene as Shakespeare presents it. Rosencrantz and Guildenstern are depicted as virtual mirror images. In response to the entreaties of the King and Queen, they offer one four-line speech apiece, each speech divided into equal syllables.

Yet whereas in Stoppard's play our previous knowledge of Rosencrantz and Guildenstern makes these recitations seem mechanical and pathetic, in *Hamlet* these two are appearing for the first time, and the impression they foster is one of proper, indeed, excessive humility. The evenness of their tone and the slickness of their language denotes a certain sinister quality. However, Gertrude's confusion with their names in lines 33–35 suggests the comic qualities that Stoppard will exploit.

The discussion with Hamlet that takes place at line 220 of act 2, scene 2 of *Hamlet* takes place largely offstage in *Rosencrantz and Guildenstern Are Dead*. Hamlet's greeting, "Good lads, how do you both" (p. 53) concludes act 1, and the final lines of the dialogue begin act 2. The scene in *Hamlet* is a series of playful puns and queries, a verbal sparring match. However, in the midst of all the imagery, Rosencrantz speaks in an aside to Guildenstern: "What say you?" (2. 2. 286). Thus nervous confusion is part of them in this play also. Otherwise, Rosencrantz and Guildenstern conduct themselves reasonably well, although they learn nothing about Hamlet's condition. With the entrance of the Players, Rosencrantz and Guildenstern step aside and are heard from no more in the scene until Hamlet leaves and Rosencrantz says "Good, my Lord" (2. 2. 532). In Stoppard's play Rosencrantz and Guildenstern leave as Polonius and the Players enter, and the pair are left to ponder what they have not learned.

Thus the differences between Shakespeare's Rosencrantz and Guildenstern and Stoppard's are twofold. First, Stoppard discards the sinister elements. Their exchanges with Hamlet go generally unheard, and the audience is left only with their befuddled impressions. Second, Stoppard magnifies the comic elements, undoubtedly present in *Hamlet*, so that the two become essentially clowns.

Throughout the rest of Stoppard's Act 2, random snatches from *Hamlet* are interspersed with Rosencrantz and Guildenstern's attempts to discover what is happening around them. For instance, Act 2, scene 2 in *Hamlet* begins as the King and Queen question Rosencrantz and Guildenstern about the success of their inquiry. In *Hamlet* the two are here on stage just briefly, and their replies bear a certain oiliness:

> QUEEN: Did he receive you well?
> Ros: Most like a gentleman.
> GUIL: But with much forcing of his disposition.
> Ros: Niggard of question, but of our demands
> Most free in his reply (3. 1. 10–13).[24]

But in the context of Stoppard's play, as Rosencrantz and Guildenstern glance hopelessly at one another, and in the context of what the audience already knows of them, the words contain more desperate inflections. A sense of hopelessness pervades the scene, of a fatalistic life where freedom is nonexistent.

The next point at which the two plays intermingle is Act 4, scene 1 of *Hamlet*, when the King shouts for Guildenstern at line 32. Both Rosencrantz and Guildenstern respond to his call in *Hamlet*. Stoppard, however, dramatizes their own confusion as to which one is Guildenstern. The King issues an order:

> Friends both, go join you with some further aid. Hamlet in madness hath Polonius slain, And from his mother's closet hath he dragged him. Go seek him out; speak fair, and bring the body Into the chapel. I pray you haste in this.
> [4. 1. 33–37]

In neither play do Rosencrantz and Guildenstern respond to this order. They simply leave. But Stoppard develops the situation. His Rosencrantz and Guildenstern are grateful for the order. As Rosencrantz says, "Well, it's *progress*, isn't it? Something positive. Seek him out" (p. 86). He takes comfort in the direction provided for him, although the two simply stand still. But Guildenstern is more disturbed: "Good God, I hope more tears are shed for *us!*" (p. 86). He is worried about the apparent amorality of the court, and he senses that he has become involved in a world where human life is worth little.

The final crossover between the two plays occurs in the very next scene of *Hamlet*, as Rosencrantz and Guildenstern urge Hamlet to show them the body and to return to the presence of the King. Hamlet completely loses the pair in his words, and in both plays he manages to disappear before them. In Shakespeare's play Rosencrantz and Guildenstern seem, however, to have kept track of Hamlet's whereabouts, and when the King so requests they have him ushered in. But in Stoppard's version Rosencrantz and Guildenstern have no idea where he has wandered, and when Hamlet does enter he does so to the grateful surprise of his schoolfellows. Again, where Shakespeare invests his two characters with a surface suavity, Stoppard depicts them as frightened, lost souls.

At the end of Act 2 of Stoppard's play, Rosencrantz and Guildenstern realize they have been assigned to escort Hamlet

to England. They do not know why, and they have no idea
if they will ever come back:

> Ros: We don't want to come back.
> Guil: That may very well be true, but do we want to go?
> [Pp. 94–95]

Theirs becomes the archetypal plight of man lost in a world
he cannot control and cannot even understand. They are
buffeted about by impersonal figures that offer a semblance
of reason and solicitude but run rampant over subjects power-
less to resist.

Before analyzing the final act of *Rosencrantz and Guildenstern Are Dead* and drawing conclusions about *Hamlet* and
the nature of theatrical absurdity, it is useful to consider the
importance of the Players in Act 2, when the Pirandellian
aspects of the play become more pronounced:

> Player: You don't understand the humiliation of it—to be tricked
> out of the single assumption which makes our exis-
> tence viable—that somebody is *watching* . [P. 63]

The sentiment provides a strong parallel in theatrical terms
to the essential predicament of absurdity. The actors need
an audience to maintain order, to inject purpose in their
lives. Otherwise their performance is just so many senseless
words and actions. Similarly Rosencrantz and Guildenstern,
representatives of humanity, require knowledge of an observer to support the meaning of their existence. This observer
traditionally has been God, and when knowledge of his presence falters, as in the condition of absurdity, then life loses
its stability.

The importance of the recourse of acting is made apparent
in the Player's next major speech:

> We're actors. . . .We pledged our identities, secure in the con-
> ventions of our trade, that someone would be watching. And
> then, gradually, no one was. We were caught, high and dry. [P. 64]

The role is thus a tool of self-determination. When an audience is observing the Players, the "act of acting" separates the Players and helps them define themselves. And at the same time that they are defining themselves, they are defining everything else in relation to them. Throughout this play the Player is perhaps the most self-assured character, equipped with a ready answer in any situation. Yet his intrinsic insecurity is apparent here, and the audience realizes that his play-acting is only a temporary respite from the crisis of absurdity. The suspicion that nobody is watching reduces the performance to a pointless charade, for then no identity is established and no separation achieved.

What is present, therefore, in the Player's desperation is the crisis of traditional absurd drama: that is, a godless world of isolation and loneliness. There is no outside society, as there is none in *Waiting for Godot* and *The Bald Soprano*. Man exists in a vacuum. And the Player's fear is that he himself will be forced to live in such a state.

Hence the importance of an audience. Hence the need for Guildenstern to plead:

> The truth is, we value your company, for want of any other. We have been left so much to our own devices—after a while one welcomes the uncertainty of being left to other people's. [P. 66]

When an outside world is part of one's life and when one can lose oneself in the machinations of that world, then losing one's own acute sense of self is, in fact, a relief from one kind of absurdity. But at the same time this escape invites another form of absurdity, which Rosencrantz and Guildenstern encounter as they try to unravel the complexities of Hamlet and his world.

The question remains how to respond to this sort of absurd world:

> GUIL: But for God's sake what are we supposed to *do*?!
> PLAYER: Relax. Respond. That's what people do. You can't go through life questioning your situation at every turn.

GUIL: But we don't know what's going on, or what to do with ourselves. We don't know how to *act*.

PLAYER: Act natural. You know why you're here at least.

GUIL: We only know what we're told, and that's little enough. And for all we know it isn't even true.

PLAYER: For all anyone knows, nothing is. Everything has to be taken on trust; truth is only that which is taken to be true. It's the currency of living. There may be nothing behind it, but it doesn't make any difference so long as it is honoured. One acts on assumptions. [Pp. 66–67]

The order to "Act natural" is a contradiction in Pirandellian terms. The word "act" implies a stylized, formalized creation, while "natural" invokes the formlessness and mutability of reality. The paradox reduces Rosencrantz and Guildenstern to the level of reaction, not action. The Player assures them that there is nothing to believe and that therefore they must be content to fabricate their own illusions. Meanwhile they should accept the directives of society and maintain that illusion that these directives are meaningful.

Thus two varieties of absurdity emerge once again. The first is man in a void, alone and left to his own devices. For Rosencrantz and Guildenstern this condition arises during those empty moments of loneliness when they are removed from the intrigues of Elsinore, when they are reduced to word games and coin flips, and when they ponder the nature of death and reflect on earlier days. The second, which emerges from the pair's meandering through the court, is the image of a man lost in a society of mysterious comings and goings, a society impossible to comprehend:

GUIL: I think I have it. A man talking sense to himself is no madder than a man talking nonsense not to himself.

Ros: Or just as mad.

GUIL: Or just as mad.

Ros: And he does both.

GUIL: So there you are.

Ros: Stark raving sane. [Pp. 67–68]

The attempt to understand that absurd world disintegrates into nonsense. And Guildenstern is aware of the collapse: "All this strolling about is getting too arbitrary by half—I'm rapidly losing my grip. From now on reason will prevail" (p. 69). It is a hopeless declaration.

The futility of rationality becomes apparent with Rosencrantz's ruminations on death. As he ponders the ramifications of lying in a box, dead, yet somehow aware of one's existence, his mind moves in minimal steps, amoeba-like, failing to tie thoughts together, simply reacting to each of his own statements as though it were disassociated from previous thoughts:

> Because you'd be helpless, wouldn't you? Stuffed in a box like that, I mean you'd be in there for ever. Even taking into account the fact that you're dead, it isn't a pleasant thought. *Especially* if you're dead, really . . .*ask* yourself, if I asked you straight off— I'm going to stuff you in this box now, would you rather be alive or dead? Naturally, you'd prefer to be alive. Life in a box is better than no life at all. I expect. You'd have a chance at least. You could lie there thinking—well, at least I'm not dead! [Pp. 70–71]

Guildenstern can only shout out in despair: "You don't have to flog it to death!" (p. 71).

But while they are searching for peace, the Court of Elsinore forbids it, and once again the royal party enters, in the context of Act 3, scene 1 of *Hamlet*. And once again, puppet-like, Rosencrantz and Guildenstern recite their appointed lines. The Player suggests the inevitability of their roles while he rehearses the mime show: "There's a design at work in all art—surely you know that? Events must play themselves out to aesthetic, moral and logical conclusion" (p. 79). Guildenstern asks a moment later, "Who decides?" And the Player's answer shocks him: "*Decides*? It is *written*" (p. 79).

The mime show itself is a further indication of Stoppard's invention. In *Hamlet* the performance is interrupted just as the murderer pours the poison in Gonzago's ear. In *Rosencrantz and Guildenstern Are Dead*, on the other hand, the entire mime is carried out in rehearsal, and its action parallels the action of *Hamlet*. Lucianus, nephew to the King, falls into the same melancholy mood as Hamlet. And two spies, dressed uncannily like Rosencrantz and Guildenstern, are victimized much as those two shall be in *Hamlet* and in Act 3 of Stoppard's play.

Clearly, two levels of meaning are at work here. On the first level is the notion of "play" itself, that Rosencrantz and Guildenstern are characters in a play which has been totally written out, and they must utter certain lines. This level, with its Pirandellian overtones, is parallel to the role they must play in society, and it therefore reinforces the concept of an outside world of absurdity which Stoppard has brought to the fore. One is reminded of the ending of *Six Characters in Search of an Author*, as the Boy is carried off dead. Some of the actors shout, "No, no, it's only make believe, it's only pretence." But the Father answers with a terrible cry: "Pretence? Reality, sir, reality!"[25] Similarly, Rosencrantz and Guildenstern are part of a larger reality over which they have no control.

The second level appears in the extra lines which Rosencrantz and Guildenstern speak when they are separated from the story of *Hamlet*. At these times they are experiencing the traditional predicament of absurdist theater. Again, Stoppard's primary accomplishment is to recognize the existence of these two levels of reality and to explore their relationship.

As there are two levels of life, so there are two levels of death. The dichotomy is made clear toward the end of Stoppard's Act 2, where the comparison is drawn between theatrical and actual death. The Player comments on Guildenstern's inquiry about death:

> It's what actors do best. They have to exploit whatever talent is given them, and their talent is dying. They can die heroically, comically, ironically, slowly, suddenly, disgustingly, charmingly, or from a great height. [P. 83]

Such is the romantic attitude toward death, or what might be called the "popular" attitude. Accordingly, death is a tragic event, cause for great sadness and momentous feeling. The view is characteristic of society and therefore of one level of absurdity, the theatrical level and the level epitomized by the plottings and counterplottings of the Court.

Guildenstern brings forth the other view of death:

> No, no, no. . .you've got it all wrong. . .you can't act death. The *fact* of it is nothing to do with seeing it happen—it's not gasps and blood and falling about—that isn't what makes it death. It's just a man failing to reappear, that's all—now you see him, now you don't, that's the only thing that's real: here one minute and gone the next and never coming back—an exit, unobtrusive and unannounced, a disappearance gathering weight as it goes on, until, finally, it is heavy with death. [P. 84]

Such is the prospect of death from the vantage point of traditional absurd theater. Once all the social conventions have been dismissed, once the traditional trappings of dignity are discarded, what remains is man's fading away. And Guildenstern's description is an ironic foreshadowing of his own death at the end of the Stoppard play.

The beginning of Act 3 reinforces the dual levels of reality and absurdity that buttress this work. Rosencrantz and Guildenstern have no idea where they are, and they attempt to locate themselves:

> Ros: We're not finished, then?
> Guil: Well, we're here, aren't we?
> Ros: Are we? I can't see a thing.
> Guil: You can still *think*, can't you?
> Ros: I think so.
> Guil: You can still *talk*.
> Ros: What should I say?
> Guil: Don't bother. You can *feel*, can't you?
> Ros: Ah! There's life in me yet! [P. 97]

This is identification at one level of absurdity, the act of determining one's existence in its purest form, irrespective of outside elements. Consequently Rosencrantz and Guildenstern proceed to establish themselves on the second level, in relation to those elements. Hearing a conglomeration of nautical terms, they deduce as follows:

> Ros: We're on a boat. (*Pause.*) Dark, isn't it?
> Guil: Not for night.
> Ros: No, not for *night*.
> Guil: Dark for day.
>   *Pause.*
> Ros: Oh yes, it's dark for *day*.
> Guil: We must have gone north, of course.
> Ros: Off course?
> Guil: Land of the midnight sun, that is.
> Ros: Of course. [Pp. 98–99]

Here they are attempting to determine the nature of the world around them, to establish the details of their environment and thereby respond in an appropriate manner. Again, this is a concession toward the second level of absurdity.

Once this task has been accomplished, Rosencrantz and Guildenstern begin to evaluate their status, and Guildenstern reflects on the nature of boats:

> Yes, I'm very fond of boats myself. I like the way they're—contained. You don't have to worry about which way to go, or whether to go at all—the question doesn't arise, because you're on a *boat*, aren't you? [Pp. 100–101]

These lines are indicative of the Pirandellian escape into form and out of mutability, for on a boat one is freed from questions of direction and self-determination. Decisions are made, and one only responds. But it is also interesting to recall George Riley's reflections on boats in *Enter a Free Man*, as he imagines himself "with home as a little boat, anchored in the middle of a big calm sea, never going anywhere, just sitting, far from land, life, everything" (p. 75). Like Guildenstern he seeks relief from the pressures of his world, and for both characters the image of floating free on water, led gently by the waves, stands as a dream to be cherished.

But simply to be aware of one's existence is insufficient. Thus Rosencrantz and Guildenstern try desperately to ascertain their purpose:

> Ros: But we've got nothing to go on, we're out on our own.
> Guil: We're on our way to England—we're taking Hamlet there.
> Ros: What for?
> Guil: What for? Where have you been? [P. 104]

They know they are headed toward England, but whether anyone will recognize them or accept them they do not know. Yet somehow they must establish themselves:

> Ros: I wish I was dead. (*Considers the drop.*) I could jump over the side. That would put a spoke in their wheel.
> Guil: Unless they're counting on it.
> Ros: I shall remain on board. That'll put a spoke in their wheel. (*The futility of it, fury.*) All right! We don't question, we don't doubt. We perform. [P. 108]

Their impotence is so frustrating. They desperately want to strike a blow against societal authority, but they are so befuddled they cannot even decide how to do any damage. They are the ultimate victims of absurdity.

Thus they can only wait and review their position. And even that, too, cannot be properly understood, for while they sleep Hamlet emerges from the shadows to steel their letter of introduction to the English king and replace it with a letter of his own. However, their lives never seem quite so precarious as with the appearance of the Players, whose now familiar flute tune assumes proportion of a *leitmotif*, symbolizing the theatrical nature of Rosencrantz and Guildstern and the fragility of their hopes.

The Player confesses that his group has left the Court of Elsinore:

> Player: In disfavour. Our play offended the King.
> Guil: Yes.

PLAYER: Well, he's a second husband himself. Tactless, really.
Ros: It was quite a good play nevertheless.
PLAYER: We never really got going—it was getting quite inter-
esting when they stopped it. [p. 115]

Their lack of vision and understanding is amusing at first,
but upon reflection it becomes pathetic. A world is functioning
around them, and they simply cannot grasp the reasons why
and how. Guildenstern attempts to put such a plight into
a somewhat optimistic perspective:

> We are not restricted. No boundaries have been defined, no inhib-
> itions imposed. We have, for the while, secured, or blundered
> into, our release, for the while. Spontaneity and whim are the
> order of the day. Other wheels are turning but they are not our
> concern. We can breathe. We can relax. We can do what we
> like and say what we like to whomever we like, without restric-
> tion. [P. 116]

But Rosencrantz shatters this dream of Pirandellian retreat
into form:

Ros: Within limits, of course.
GUIL: Certainly within limits. [P. 116]

However, such "limited freedom" is no substitute for knowledge. And the frustrations Rosencrantz and Guildenstern
feel at being pawns in the hands of such a world are epitomized
by Rosencrantz's cry: "Incidents! All we get is incidents!
Dear God, is it too much to expect a little sustained action?!"
(p. 118). His is a plea for an end to absurdity. One of the sal-
ient characteristics of absurd theater is that the plays are
devoid of order, thereby reduced to a series of free-floating
images. Rosencrantz's life has been a similar catalogue of
disorder, and he is searching for some thread of order to bring
meaning to these apparently random events.

Unfortunately, the reverse takes place, and when Hamlet
disappears after the pirates' attack, the focal point of their
lives leaves with him:

> GUIL (*near tears*): Nothing will be resolved without him. . .
> PLAYER: There. . . !
> GUIL: We need Hamlet for our release!
> PLAYER: There!
> GUIL: What are we supposed to do? [P. 120]

Hamlet was a constant element, the one clear reality that they recognized. Even if they failed to understand the complications he aroused, still they knew that their place was with him, and thus their lives had meaning. Now they exist totally in a void:

> GUIL: (*broken*) We've travelled too far, and our momentum has taken over; we move idly towards eternity, without possibiltiy of reprieve or hope of explanation. [P. 121]

Given the dead end that their life has become, Guildenstern remains determined to establish his existence. He is resolved not to pass from the earth without somehow mattering. The Player comments on the uselessness of it all: "In our experience, most things end in death" (p. 123). But Guildenstern will not allow himself to be compared with the ephemeral, make-believe roles of the actors. Therefore in frustration he stabs the Player, who pretends to die with elaborate histrionics. Guildenstern insists on the significance of his act:

> If we have a destiny, then so had he—and if this is ours, then that was his—and if there are no explanations for us, then let there be none for him— [P. 123]

He has attempted to commit the sheer gratuitous act. If life persists in its senselessness, he will respond accordingly, by behaving without reason and without regard for conventional morality. It is useful to compare Guildenstern's attempt at murder with Meursault's murder of the Arab in Camus' *The Stranger*. Meursault's first shot with the revolver is accidental, but he insists on firing four more times into the lifeless body in order to accept responsibility for the act and to insist on his independence from the universe. Meursault achieves his end. But Guildenstern is denied that satisfaction, for the Player stands up, revealing the futility of Guildenstern's effort to counteract absurdity.

The Players complete the mime, as the two "spies" dressed as Rosencrantz and Guildenstern are stabbed amidst the Player's romantic interpretation of death. But Guildenstern reaffirms his conviction about the nature of death in an absurd world:

> No. . .no. . .not for *us*, not like that. Dying is not romantic, and death is not a game which will soon be over. . .Death is not anything. . .death is not. . .It's the absence of presence, nothing more. . . the endless time of never coming back. . .a gap you can't see, and when the wind blows through it, it makes no sound. [P. 124]

And that is how they disappear, as confused as ever, wondering just how they went wrong. The manner of their death is much like the final moments of King Berenger in Ionesco's *Exit the King,* who is described as "fading into a kind of mist" (p. 95). But Berenger exists on only one level of absurdity, and no world survives around him. When Rosencrantz and Guildenstern die, that outside world that they had tried to comprehend, the Court of Elsinore, that society continues the recitation of blank verse, oblivious to their death. Guildenstern's earlier fear, "I hope more tears are shed for *us*!. . ." (p. 86) proves prophetic.

Two concluding issues need to be resolved. First, what is the status of *Hamlet* at the end of *Rosencrantz and Guildenstern Are Dead?* Above all, it has been invested with a number of theatrical characteristics traditionally not ascribed to it. Its plot is seen as but a fragmented series of events. Its characters are one-dimensional, scrambling about the stage with no apparent sense, motivation, or emotional depth of any sort. Its language has been humbled to the level of nonsense. The noble poetry is now so much bombast which does not promote communication but rather blocks it. On a more intimate level, the world of *Hamlet* is one without morality. The King murders his brother with no twinge of remorse, at least none indicated here. Hamlet kills Polonius by mistake, and he dispatches Rosencrantz and Guildenstern with cold calculation. The Players are content to let their youngest member prostitute himself for their money. The only two characters who demonstrate any ethics are Rosencrantz and Guildenstern.

The question then arises as to what extent life is of any value at all, even in Shakespeare's *Hamlet*, and how seriously the murders and deaths are to be taken. In the first of the mime shows which mirror the events of Elsinore, Gonzago is killed when poison is poured in his ear, a death surely not befitting royalty and bordering on the ridiculous. In succeeding mimes bodies drop on all sides with stunning suddenness. The effect has elements of slapstick comedy, and when Rosencrantz and Guildenstern are reported dead, the court is moved only to think of them as two more bodies. The audience is presented with no sense of love in this world and little sense of loss at death. The natural and royal order is restored as Fortinbras gains power, and life moves on inexorably.

When all these considerations are taken together, the result is that *Hamlet* has been transformed into an absurd play. And that conclusion gives rise to the final critical judgment about *Rosencrantz and Guildenstern Are Dead*. Stoppard begins his play in the world of traditional absurd theater, recalling specifically Beckett's *Waiting for Godot*. But he brings his characters into a new world, one where elements of absurdity are disguised under a mask of order and reason worn by a society which Stoppard has made us come to see as perhaps absurd itself. Within this society Stoppard develops the concept of role-playing in Pirandellian terms, so that his now realistic figures are aware of the theatrical, hence precarious, nature of their existence.

Thus Stoppard has created two levels of absurdity: the

recently traditional one, where men have no role to play and must fabricate reasons for their existence, and a second one, within an incomprehensible society, where men play a role that is strictly defined but still hopelessly unfathomable. This double layer provides a dimension new in absurd theater, and in his next plays Stoppard will explore the various ramifications of this development and expand it even further.

3/Stoppard's Fiction

Although the subject of this book is the creative development of Tom Stoppard in his drama, it is useful to consider his creativity and attitudes in his fiction, which consists of a novel, *Lord Malquist and Mr. Moon*, and three short stories available in publication. Correspondencies appear both in the concepts and in the manipulation of the two fictional genres.

Lord Malquist and Mr. Moon (1966)

Lord Malquist and Mr. Moon has been called "a *tour de force* of absurdist fiction,"[1] and it is particularly intriguing to study in the light of Stoppard's early plays. For in this novel several of the same themes are developed according to a different perspective and, as such, they foreshadow many of the plays to follow.

Basic characteristics of absurd theater have been transferred to this work of fiction. Most apparent is the general disjointed structure, composed of a series of incidents and images tied together by a single group of characters and a few recurrent themes. Furthermore, the book presents no sense of plot development, exposition, or climax, and the time sequence is irregular. The setting is apparently in the twentieth century, but more specific detail is uncertain.

As in absurd drama, this dramatic structure reflects the vision of a fragmented, irrational world, an attitude embellished by the tone, one of blanked-out emotion. Incredible and sometimes horrific events are reported with vacuous tranquility, making at times for a sort of black humor. For instance, at the very end of the novel, when an explosion has destroyed the coach in which Mr. Moon is riding, the result is explained as "dispersing Moon and O'Hara and bits of pink and yellow wreckage at various points along the road between the Palace and Parliament Square."[2]

More important, however, than structural comparisons are the thematic similarities between this novel and Stoppard's plays. What is presented in *Lord Malquist and Mr. Moon* is a world as confusing and incomprehensible as the one which surrounds George Riley (the "Free Man") and the court that surrounds Rosencrantz and Guildenstern. The world is one of violence, chaos, and hopeless complexity. This concept is emphasized constantly, proving to be the foundation for whatever rational action the novel depicts:

> Moon tried to seal off his mind against his integrality with a vast complex of moving parts all dependent on each other and maintained on the brink of disintegration only by their momentum. [P. 19]

> "Such utter disregard for the common harmonies of life," complained the ninth earl. "I look around me and I recoil from such disorder. We live amidst absurdity, so close to it that it escapes our notice. But if the sky were turned into a great mirror and we caught ourselves in it unawares, we should not be able to look each other in the face." [P. 21]

A conflict familiar from Stoppard's other works is thereby set up: how is man to reconcile himself to that absurd world in which he has been placed?

The answers to this question form the content of the novel. On the one hand is the attitude of Lord Malquist, "the ninth earl," whose strategy is stated clearly: "Since we cannot hope for order let us withdraw with style from the chaos" (p. 21). The opposite stance is that of Mr. Moon, who strives in various ways to struggle against the chaos of absurdity and to formulate some social, intellectual, and moral order. Between these two viewpoints are other manners of approaching the world, which range from sheer escape to attempts at bringing purpose to a universe of seemingly random chance.

The essence of Lord Malquist's position is made apparent in the very first paragraph of the novel:

> "When the battle becomes a farce the only position of dignity is above it," said the ninth earl (the battle raging farcically beneath him). "On the day the Bastille fell Louis XVI of France returned home from the hunt and wrote in his private diary, *Rien.* I comment to you the dignity of that remark, not to mention its cosmic accuracy." [P. 8]

The rest of the paragraph describes in detail Malquist's apparel and accessories. Throughout the novel he is preoccupied with particularities of dress and furniture, losing his sense of the absurdity of the world in his concern over trivia. He concedes that life is meaningless, therefore invents his own world of meaning through a concession to a life as a "Stylist—the spectator as hero, the man of inaction who would not dare roll up his sleeves for fear of creasing his cuffs" (p. 79). As a result, he has dispensed with all morality and feeling for human life. For instance, at the end of the first section of the novel he accidentally runs down a woman in his coach. His only reaction is to comment, "Breeding. . .as Lord Curzon said to the actress, a lady does not move" (p. 12). And he pops a chocolate into his mouth. The events of the world leave him absolutely unperturbed.

It is useful to compare Lord Malquist to the Player in *Rosencrantz and Guildenstern Are Dead.* Both seek release from absurdity in the form of theatrical posture. The Player takes refuge in literal dramatics, the Lord in the theatrics of life and style. Both are transformed from participants into detached observers of life.

Other recourses from accepting the plight of absurdity are demonstrated by a man known as "The Risen Christ" and by Moon's wife. The Risen Christ is encountered early in the book when he appears with his donkey by a lake. In

Stoppard's description he shares all the attributes of the pro-
phets of old, complete with beard, bare feet, and linen robe.
His mind works at first in a spirit of deep religious conviction:

> He was tired and very hungry. He hoped to find a fig-tree among
> the stunted hawthorns but there was food only for the donkey.
> He smiled gently at this reminder of the infinite workings that
> compensated all God's creatures for their limitations and checked
> them for their presumptions. [P. 14]

Yet by the end of the scene, after he has urged his donkey
to move along, the Risen Christ is reduced to kicking the
animal in the genitals, cursing and beating at it. As the novel
develops the man is revealed to be a figure of dubious morality,
who has responded to his world by taking haven in the guise
of religious sanctity. Once again Stoppard offers a character
who escapes into theatrical form rather than confront absurdity.

Moon's wife, named Jane, does not retreat into a role so
much as into herself, delighting in her own body and reveling
in a perpetual sensuality. She exists to move from bed to bath
and back, in the company of her parade of lovers. Stoppard
describes her actions as she imagines Scotsmen in their kilts:

> Her hands flat-ironed the peacock shine of her thighs, smoothed
> upwards against her stomach and down dragging splay-fingered
> against the groin, clawed and dug and furrowed palm-to-palm
> into the hollow and parted, stretching the silk over her bottom
> and back, gathering it into the soft of her waist and climbed again,
> moulding her rib-cage, pushed high her breasts and flattened
> them into the V of her throat. [Pp. 61–62]

The sensuality is carried to the ridiculous. Nothing is actually
happening, but Jane's preoccupation with sensation serves as a
substitute for thought. Throughout the novel Jane remains un-
moved by events outside her bedroom, whether it be the murder of one of her cowboy suitors or that of her maid Marie. Hers
is total asylum from reality and its corollary, absurdity. She

denies all that is not specifically devoted to her own bodily pleasures.

The major character in this novel, and the one whose reaction to the world forms the basis of whatever narrative structure is established, is Mr. Moon. His immediate role in life is secretary to Lord Malquist, and his responsibility is to copy down all the Lord's pronouncements on life, government, fashion, and the nature of existence. For Lord Malquist the act of dictation is part of his general theatrics, his desire for "style" in the face of meaninglessness. But for Moon the act of recording is one of counteracting that absurdity:

> He stood for peace of mind. For tidiness. For control, direction order; proportion, above all he stood for proportion. Quantities—volume and number—must be related to the constant of the human scale, proportionate. [P. 63]

Earlier he attempted to write a history of the world, to arrange all the events that seemed incomprehensible into a rational order, to grasp the random actions and link them in a chain of cause and effect. But the hopelessness of the project overwhelmed him, and he managed only a few opening sentences which were thrown away in despair. Yet the disorder of the world still confounds him. Thus he has undertaken the role of Boswell to Lord Malquist's Dr. Johnson, only to become aware of his own inadequacies in that role. He constantly forgets dialogue when he tries to write down the day's proceedings, and his diary, what little there is of it, is nothing but a compendium of vapid trivia. The final indignity is the last sentence of his opening chapter:

> Tomorrow I hope to do better justice to Lord Malquist's conversation—I did in fact make some notes today but unfortunately my notebook was destroyed in a small fire later on. [P. 101]

Jill Levenson notes that, like many of Beckett's characters, Moon suffers physical torments that mirror his psychological and metaphysical pain.[3] Early in the novel he accidentally cuts his face and arm. He acquires a wound in the bottom of his foot which becomes steadily more infected, and throughout the novel he must wipe blood away from the wound. From time to time he even loses some feeling in his legs, a state symbolic of his lack of ability to function in the world. At one point Moon is so driven to frustration that he scrambles as best he can about his house, turning on all the taps, fixtures, and machines. One is reminded of Guildenstern's attempted murder of the Player. In a world of absurdity, where reason is alien, the only way to rebel is to act without reason, to match the world's condition with a series of senseless actions of one's own.

Between Moon and Malquist there is a good deal of talk *about* absurdity. For that absurdity to be meaningful, however, it must be *dramatized*. In this novel absurdity is dramatized most effectively through constant accounts of death and destruction, always accepted with utter calm. For instance, the background event of the story is the funeral of what appears to have been a national hero. As mentioned earlier, Lord Malquist kills a woman as he drives his coach. Moon himself murders a general. Marie, Jane's maid, is accidentally shot by a cowboy and lies untouched for an extended time. That cowboy, Long John Slaughter, is continually threatening to have a shoot-out with another cowboy named Jasper Jones. As if to symbolize the significance of this bombardment of violence, a roll of paper is seen from time to time unfolding. It seems to bear the connotations of a knowledge-giving scroll but turns out to be toilet paper, a mock version of holy scripture.

The novel is also permeated with an unusual number of references to animals and various bodily functions. Lord Malquist has equipped himself with two trained pets, a hawk and a lion, that carry out his violent desires which he suppresses under the guise of ritual. Even Lord Malquist's first name, Falcon, denotes a vicious hunting bird. The Risen Christ's donkey appears sporadically, transforming itself into a parody of that character's sanctimonious pronouncements.

The emphasis on animalism becomes more pronounced amidst the plethora of body imagery. Mrs. Moon, nicknamed "Fertility Jane" by Long John Slaughter, is, as indicated, a creature devoted to her own anatomy. But the text is elsewhere saturated with body imagery. For instance, in the passages of sexual activity, the suggestion is not of expressions of love, but rather, in the tradition of absurdity, of biological necessity. As Moon himself reflects, after his initial encounter with Lady Malquist, the first sexual experience of his life, "He thought that he might after all get through life if he could periodically (two or three times a day) rendez-vous with Lady Malquist for his sexual fix" (p. 145). The description of their love-making is appropriately animalistic:

> She drew him through the curtain folds and laid him down in soft grey light, her fingers sinuous and busy about him, her mouth fish-feeding on his, and turned under him with underwater grace and gripped hard making sea-moans that lingered in the flooded chambers of his mind where all his fears separated into seaweed strands and flowed apart and were gone as he clung with his limbs and his mouth to sanctuary. [P. 143]

Lord Malquist dictates a letter to the *Times* while crawling about the bathtub with Moon's wife: "His head sank lower and one of his legs emerged dripping leprous from the foam" (p. 76).

The combination of bodily imagery mixed with animal references reduces the human activity in this novel to a bestial level. The effect is that of creatures moving from one physical response to another, reacting not with their minds and emotions but with their bodies to various environmental stimuli. The dehumanization is steady and powerful.

Given this state of the world, its inevitable violence, and its absurdity, Moon cannot aim for reformation. Thus he resolves otherwise: "It needs an explosion to shock people into calling a halt and catch up, stop and recognize, *realize*—everyone takes it all for granted" (p. 18). Like Rosencrantz and Guildenstern, his only comfort is a few memories. That pair dwells upon their

home and the times when their lives were peaceful. Moon
remembers his Uncle Jackson, a scientist, who was able to bring
a measure of order to the world. In one of the few tranquil
moments of the novel, Moon recalls the innocence of that boy-
hood memory:

> I used to walk through woods in summer with all the leaves in
> place, which was very nice, and in the autumn too, shushing
> through beds of leaves, but once I was lying on my back under a
> tree looking at a leaf and just as I was looking at it, it slipped off
> the tree, without a sound or warning, it just came away and dropped
> down on me. Yellow. A chestnut leaf. I like things like that, catching
> the instant between the continuing things, because when you
> actually see a leaf come away like that then you know about
> summer and autumn, properly.[P. 138]

This passage is particularly important, for it reveals all that is
missing from Moon's world now. He has lost touch with innocence. He has been unable to find refuge in nature. He has been
unable to find solitude. And, most of all, he has been unable
to find order, a rational progression of cause and effect. Therefore his world has become incomprehensible and intolerable.

Moon tries to explain his confusion in much the way that
Rosencrantz and Guildenstern do. They continually summarize
their situation, tying everything together in what they hope
will prove to be a rational set of circumstances. The last time
they do so is on the boat, just before they go to sleep and before
Hamlet switches letters with them (p. 111). Similarly, Moon
attempts to correlate the sequences around him (p. 150), but he
can only conclude that, "It was as if he were the victim of a
breathtaking conspiracy instituted at his birth, leading him
from one planned encounter to another" (p. 151).

The final insult is his realization that he has been deserted
by both his wife, Jane, who through the course of the novel
acquires several lovers, and then his mistress, Lady Malquist.
He attempts to calm himself by taking a ride in a coach, but
he is mistaken for Lord Malquist by Mr. Cuttle, an anarchist
and husband of the woman who had been run over in the first

scene of the novel. Cuttle throws a bomb which blows up the coach and Moon with it. His death is as irrational as his life. Throughout the novel he has been carrying his own bomb with him, ready to throw it as an ultimate gesture of defiance against an unsympathetic world. But Moon is denied even that minor triumph.

The thematic parallels between *Lord Malquist and Mr. Moon* and the two early full-length plays of Stoppard are clear. In all three the protagonists are befuddled victims of the world around them. But the novel also continues important thematic development. In *Enter a Free Man* the structure is essentially realistic, with only intimations of absurdity. In *Rosencrantz and Guildenstern Are Dead* absurdity is confronted, but on two different levels: the level of personal identity and metaphysical loneliness, and that of the confusion of outside society. In *Lord Malquist and Mr. Moon* absurdity is encountered almost totally on the second level. Moon remains a lost figure, pondering, arranging, and cataloguing episodes but unable to formulate any order. His anguish, his suicidal thoughts, his pathetic memories, all are in the tradition of the absurd to which Stoppard has brought a new dramatic level first explored in *Rosencrantz and Guildenstern Are Dead.*

"Reunion"; "Life, Times: Fragments"; "The Story" (1964)

These three short stories stand as unusual Stoppard works. The first reason is obvious; they are his only three short stories. But a more important reason is their tone, one of sober, at times bitter, reflection.

"Reunion"

"Reunion" concerns a nameless, apparently middle-aged man, who comes by surprise to visit an old girl friend, now married and living a drab, spiritless existence. As they sit next to one another at her kitchen table, they scarely know what to say or do; yet obvious tensions arise. As he probes her present life, she protests, "Oh, please, there's no point."[4]

Between bits of small talk he gradually reveals his reason for coming, or rather his lack of reason for going anywhere else. In a confession analogous to the plight of Mr. Moon, the man begins, "I don't know what to do" (p. 122). He continues to explain:

> "There is a certain word," he said very carefully, "which if shouted at the right pitch and in a silence worthy of it, would nudge the universe into gear. You understand me, it would have to be shouted in some public place dedicated to silence, like the reading room at the British Museum, it must violate it, a monstrous, unspeakable intrusion after which nothing can be the same for the man who does it." [p. 123]

The speech is a plea for order, a desire for the soulless, mechanistic processes of the world to stop completely for an instant so that the protagonist may at least once be able to ascertain his position. Like Mr. Moon, who continually threatens to explode a bomb to bring the world to its senses, so the nameless protagonist wants to achieve the same effect with a single shouted word, though he confesses to be unsure what that word might be, or even whether it is part of a recognized language.

He does, however, remember an occasion when a small portion of his world was brought to attention:

> "We were remembering the dead, supposed to be. At school, in the town church we went to, six hundred of us suspended in the thick of the two-minute silence, and I knocked my prayer-book off the ledge. It hit the floor flat and went off like a pistol shot. I reckon for two seconds everything intrusive to my self flew out of me, and then back." [P. 124]

After relating this incident he tries to frighten his former girl friend into rejoining him: "Listen, he'll beat you. He'll come home drunk on Friday nights and beat you and your children will cry between their damp sheets to the sound of breaking crockery" (p. 124). After he confesses that what he really misses is the warmth of their relationship, the woman demurs, insisting lamely on her present happiness. In short, desperate sentences characteristic of Pinteresque dialogue, the pair's loneliness is apparent, but always understated, as the attempt at reestablishing their relationship fails.

The story concludes with the man's departing, still lonely and lost. In miniature, Stoppard has presented his most important theme: that of man wandering about a world that he cannot understand. No details of that world are provided. Even the century is indeterminate. But once again there are intimations of an absurd universe, impersonal, cold, and characterized by a menace bordering on terror.

"Life, Times: Fragments"

Loneliness amidst an inscrutable world is also the theme of "Life, Times: Fragments." The story is structured in a series of short passages, from the points of view alternately of an aspiring writer and an omniscient narrator.

The first two paragraphs deal with the writer's experience with newspapers. He blunders on his first assignment, unknowingly reporting a woman dead when she is still alive. Finally she does die, and he feels oddly relieved. When he is rejected for a job as a political reporter for not knowing the name of the Foreign Secretary, he resolves to turn to fiction: "Then I can make the Foreign Secretary anybody I bloody well like" (p. 127). Stymied by reality, he retreats into his own world, attempting to foster meaning in life through art.

But his writing, demonstrated to us in succeeding paragraphs, is poor and imitative. The first passage is an attempt to capture the style of Hemingway, the tight-lipped voice of an emotionless adventurer:

It had taken me ten days to get that far, from Avignon where they dropped me off. I had a bad time to Narbonne and in the square after the cafe closed it rained through the plane trees and the lights of heavy lorries swung big and yellow through the rain going south, but in the morning it was hot walking over the bridge and down the long straight between the vineyards. [P. 127]

The next paragraph suggests that his writing career has, not surprisingly, failed: "Shouting into the teeth of the thirty-fourth year of his obscurity, he patrolled the battleground of fallen heroes, skillfully shooting the wounded" (p. 127). In other words, he strives to alleviate the pain of his failure by tearing down more successful writers. "Listen," he said, "the models are no good any more, we've had all that, we're on our own now" (p. 128). He is the first of Stoppard's characters to attempt to escape from a world that rejects him by seeking recourse in absolute artistic freedom and individualism.

But in the next passage his supposed attempts at individuality also turn out to be mere imitation, this time of Samuel Beckett's novels. The narrative proceeds in the convoluted fashion of one man's tenuous rationality:

I am seriously thinking of getting up now. Something is troubling me, however. I cannot remember whether I forgot to say my prayers last night or whether I decided not to. It might make a difference if there is any difference to be made. . . . Do not despair: one of the thieves was saved. Do not presume: one of the thieves was damned. [P. 128]

The parallel to Beckett is reinforced by the quotation from St. Augustine for which Beckett has expressed much admiration:

There is a wonderful sentence in Augustine. I wish I could remember the Latin. It is even finer in Latin than in English. "Do not despair: one of the thieves was saved. Do not presume: one of the thieves was damned."[5]

Vladimir in *Waiting for Godot* ponders these same lines (pp. 8–9).

The writer's career goes nowhere, and eventually he surrenders his ambitions. In his rejection of society he overcomes his doubts about the existence of God and turns heavenward for solace amid the world he cannot conquer:

> Falling on his knees, he cried out loud, joyfully, "Dear Lord, I have seen the Light. Forgive my former pride and witness my humility. I cast off my worldly aspirations, and offer myself, Dear Lord, wholly to your eternal service." And the Lord heard him and He sent an angel to the writer as he knelt, and the angel said, "The Lord thanks you for your contribution but regrets that it is not quite suitable for the Kingdom of Heaven." [P. 129]

He is the only Stoppard character ever to place his trust in God, and the answer he receives is as cold and impersonal as his treatment at the hands of the world.

The writer commits suicide, and in the last paragraph his body and suicide note are discovered by a famous critic, who is taken with the writing: "It is my considered etcetera bitter humour Gogol agonized vision Kafkacetera etcetera" (p. 130). The critical jargon is nonsense, but so is a world where values and taste are such variables. The critic manages to make the writer famous, at the same time furthering his own career.

This story reflects Stoppard's concern with lonely, rejected figures trying to achieve a place in the world. In addition, this is the first of his works founded on parody and literary allusion, techniques which become extremely important in later works such as *Artist Descending a Staircase* and *Travesties*.

"The Story"

The plot of "The Story" is simple. A newspaper reporter for a press service covers an out-of-town court session. The final case is one of child molestation, and the reporter promises the defendant that the story will not be publicized, but one of his associates insists the details be sent along to the wire service. The narrating reporter is later called for additional information, and he eventually tells all that he knows. A week after the story is published, the defendant, a schoolteacher named Blake, commits suicide. Again his story makes the papers.

The theme is another one integral to Stoppard's writing: that of the manipulation of the individual by society and the individual's inability to control his own destiny. The narrator/reporter attempts to control events around him, and that conflict is set up in the second paragraph:

> There are P.S. staff-men in all the big places and a load of stringers everywhere else. They send in anything worth sending, and when Diver is out of town—he has the whole county and a bit more—the *Sun* Office stands in for him. [P. 131]

An anonymous power determines the pattern of the news, and the narrator as much as admits his own incapacity.

But the narrator's powerlessness is paralleled in more subtle fashion by Blake's:

> The bloke was pleading guilty. He was red and tweedy and too fat but the main thing about him was that he kept grinning. I really mean grinning but there was nothing there. It was just a shape he put his mouth into. He was too fat and altogether sick with where he had got himself. [P. 132]

Blake seems to seek the role of victim, perhaps of sexual drives that forced him to molest the little girl. These might be likened to the private level of absurdity. But Blake also endures victimization at the hands of outside society. For when details of the case reach the newspaper office, the story arouses interest and is published, accompanied by a picture and some quotations from authorities. One week later Blake jumps in front of a moving train.

The narrator's tone throughout is impassive. He notes coldly that some newspapers had found a couple of new pictures of the dead Blake, but "the *Chronicle* had one of his fiancée, which was a beat [sic] because no one knew he had one" (p. 136). His words carry no sympathy for the woman or the victim. And a few days later, when the case is recalled, the newspapermen have forgotten who Blake was. The world goes on, and the narrator's only comment is that he was "broke as usual" (p. 136).

In this brief piece Stoppard has dramatized the plight of two characters, completely unrelated, who nonetheless suffer the same fate: that of submission to a world that functions beyond their control. The story is virtually humorless but still tinged with absurdity, and it is an effective portrait of man trapped in the power of a system.

In addition, this is the first of Stoppard's writings in which the system assumes characteristics of contemporary society, the impersonal processes that determine our life patterns. In several of his shorter plays, to be analyzed presently, he explores other social institutions in terms of absurd theater. Previously, complex social sturctures were alien to that theater, but Stoppard succeeds in creating this new dimension, and his results are worth study.

4/Stoppard's One-Act, Television, and Radio Plays

Of Tom Stoppard's many one-act plays for stage, television, and radio, eleven are available in publication.[1] I shall discuss eight in this chapter.

If You're Glad I'll Be Frank (1966)

This radio play, first broadcast 8 February 1966, reinforces the conflict between levels of absurdity that Stoppard has developed in previous plays. However, in this work that second level of absurdity, the level of the outside world and society's incomprehensible processes, is no longer a befogged suspicion as in *Enter a Free Man*. Nor is it the distant Elizabethan court, as in *Rosencrantz and Guildenstern Are Dead*. Nor is it placed in the uncertain time frame of *Lord Malquist and Mr. Moon*. For the first time in a Stoppard play the absurd world depicted is quite clearly contemporary and recognizable. Man is no longer a mere victim of vague processess. He now encounters a concrete force against which to fight back, although he is still losing.

The dual structure of absurdity, and consequently of the world itself, is shaped at the very opening of the play. Frank calls up the telephone company to learn the exact time. In the voice answering he recognizes the intonations of his wife, Gladys, mindlessly reciting the precise time every ten seconds. In the printed text Stoppard has taken pains to separate his two levels by providing parallel speaking columns. Throughout the play, when the text is so formed, one column represents Gladys's oral recitations. The other represents her own inner thoughts while speaking. One column is thus her role in society, the other her own identity independent of social patterns.

The next scene depicts the absurd world itself. Since this is a radio play, such depiction must rely solely on the sounds of voices and objects. Stoppard develops the mechanical sense of his absurd by synchronizing the opening and closing of the building doors with the stroking of Big Ben. The dialogue is nothing but perfunctory greetings, rhythmic and machine-like:

> PORTER: Morning, Mrs. Trelawney.
> MYRTLE (*gay*): Hello, Tommy.
>   (*And out through door.*)
>   (*Street door.*)
> PORTER: Morning, Mr. Mortimer.
> MORTIMER (*tired*): Good morning, Tom.
>   (*And out through door.*)
>   (*Street door.*)[2]

At this point it would be useful to consider the various ramifications of the use of radio as a dramatic medium. In this play the stage would be somewhat of a hindrance, for the story moves from scene to scene with a fluidity that would be much less effective in a theater. More important, the interior monologues of Gladys, which form the bases of many of the succeeding scenes, are particularly appropriate to radio. For instance, scene three creates the stream-of-consciousness pattern of Gladys' mind as she is reciting the time at ten-second intervals. The narrative technique is especially eerie, as the listener loses sense of all external elements and maintains contact only with the human voice, thus creating for himself the sense of a mind rolling uncontrollably in thought.

This passage in scene three is also thematically significant in its relation to the rest of Stoppard's writing. The focus of the reflection is the nature of time, its problematic role in human life. Gladys begins by pondering the artificiality of human existence:

```
Because they think that
    time is something they
    invented,
for their own convenience . . .
So that they'd know how
    long they lasted,
and pretend that it matters,
and how long they've got,
as if it mattered,
so that they'd know that we
    know that they know. [Pp. 44–45]
```

Her words cut through to one of the fundamental quandaries of man's existence: the inevitable frustration of trying to stop time and bring organization to life. In the very act of focusing on the individual man at an individual moment, we must lose track, as that moment passes immediately. And, simultaneously, the act of such focusing makes the viewer aware of the meaninglessness of life:

```
When you look down from
    a great height
you become dizzy. Such
    depth, such distance,
such disappearing tininess so
    far away,
rushing away,
reducing the life-size to
nothing—
it upsets the scale you live by. [P. 45].
```

Perpetual contemplation of the passing time, the great pageant of history, leaves the viewer lost in a time coulisse.

Passages such as this one inevitably bring to mind the writings of Samuel Beckett. In his critical study *Proust* Beckett attempts to analyze this tormenting aspect of human existence:

There is no escape from the hours and the days. Neither from tomorrow nor from yesterday. There is no escape from yesterday because yesterday has deformed us, or been deformed by us.[3]

Richard Coe notes that what Beckett discovered in Proust was "an attempt to resolve the conflict between 'awareness,' which is instantaneous, and the linear extension in time of that same awareness when translated into language."[4] Thus man's inability to ascertain the past—Krapp's predicament in *Krapp's Last Tape*. The past is but "an image as far removed from the real as the myth of our imagination or the caricature furnished by direct perception."[5] Memory, the past, and, consequently, each individual self lie hopelessly beyond comprehension. And under such circumstances, as Gladys notes:

> . . .time viewed from
>   such distance
> etcetera
> rushing away
> reducing the lifespan to
>   nothing
> and so on— [P. 46]

While Gladys reflects on the hopelessness of perceiving the individual mind, Frank battles equally hopelessly against the maze of systems that compose society. In scene four he manages once again to reach the voice of Gladys routinely reciting the time, and even that minor triumph causes him to shout with joy: "I've found my Gladys!" (p. 47). He resolves to rescue her from imprisonment.

Meanwhile, Gladys ruminates on the futility of her position. In a passage reminiscent of Rosencrantz and Guildenstern, she imagines:

> If it made a difference
> I could refuse to play,
> sabotage the whole illusion
> a little every day if it made a
>   difference,
> as if it would, if I coughed or
>   jumped a minute. . .
> And if stopped altogether,

just stopped, gave up the pretence,
it would make no difference.
Silence is the sound of time passing. [Pp. 50–51]

Just as Rosencrantz and Guildenstern try to upset the plans
of their world on the boat but are frustrated by their ignorance
of just what action might "put a spoke in their wheel" (p. 108),
so Gladys realizes that whatever she does might cause momen-
tary confusion but ultimately would make no difference at
all. Time would pass, as ever. "It's never the time that stops"
(p. 51).

To escape her concern with time and nature of identity,
Gladys indulges in that preoccupation characteristic of absurdist figures such as Krapp: the retreat into memory and the
joyous experiences of the past:

> Yes, we met dancing. I liked him
>   from the first.
> He said, "If you're Glad
> I'll be Frank. . ."
> There was time to laugh then
> but while I laughed a bumblebee
> fluttered its wings a million times.
> How can one compete?. . .
> Old Frank. He had all the time
> in the world for me,
> such as it was. [Pp. 52–53]

Like Krapp, she abandons the memory. Even its pleasures are
fleeting in the shadow of the infinite movement of the bumble-
bee's wings.

Gladys also maintains memories of lost illusions:

> I was going to be a nun, but they wouldn't have me because I
> didn't believe. I didn't believe *enough*, that is; most of it I believed
> all right, or was willing to believe, but not enough for their pur-
> poses, not about him being the son of God, for instance, that's
> the part that put paid [sic] to my ambition, that's where we didn't

see eye to eye. . . .I asked her to let me stay inside without being a proper nun, it made no difference to me, it was the serenity I was after, that and the clean linen, but she wasn't having any of that. [Pp. 56–57]

Unable to accept belief in a divine world order, she nonetheless desires escape from the chaos and absurdity of outside society and into the monastery, where in Pirandellian style she could play a pre-determined role and be free from the need to act on her own. Instead, she is thrust back into the absurdity. Now her mind gradually disintegrates, and she giggles madly at the thought of whispering an obscenity into the phone, one "that will leave ten thousand coronaries sprawled across their telephone tables" (p. 61). Like Guildenstern, like Mr. Moon, she needs to perform a gratuitous act that will demonstrate her scorn for the conventions of an absurd world.

Meanwhile Frank battles against the mechanized world. But as a bus driver he is tied to his schedule and constantly interrupted in his quest by orders to return to the road. When he finally succeeds in reaching the front of the building where Gladys works, he meets further opposition:

> PORTER: You can't park there after seven if the month's got an R in it or before nine if it hasn't except on Christmas and the Chairman's birthday should it fall in Lent. [P. 53]

Eventually he bullies his way through a series of obstacles to meet at last with the First Lord of the Post Office, but the war is lost when the Lord fools him into believing that Glady's voice is only a recording. After Frank leaves, the Lord speaks in person to Gladys, calms her down, and restores her to mechanistic efficiency. Her surrender is the total victimization of humanity by automation.

Jill Levenson has written of "the tension between Gladys's hard-won individuality and the programmed role she is forced to play"[6] This dichotomy of personality is essentially the same one that characterizes Rosencrantz and Guildenstern, based on two levels of absurdity. Frank, too, functions on two levels, although he is much more concerned with that second level, the relationship between the individual and the society surrounding him. In this play, and in several plays to follow, Stoppard brings to that level specific characteristics of contemporary society in an effort to depict man moving from out of the depths of loneliness and into an active confrontation with society.

A Separate Peace (1966)

The desire for retreat from absurdity is dramatized movingly in *A Separate Peace*, a one-act television play first transmitted 22 August 1966. The protagonist, John Brown, registers at a hospital, not because of any illness, but just because, he says, "I need a place to stay."[7] As he explains, "It's the privacy I'm after—that and clean linen" (p. 108). The hospital system is befuddled by his request but admits him while trying to conceive a reason to expel him.

The crucial point of the drama is Brown's reason for pursuing refuge. He confesses he has no family, just a sufficient amount of money. When asked why he chose a hospital, rather than a hotel, he answers:

> I want to do nothing, and have nothing expected of me. That isn't possible out there. It worries them. They want to know what you're at—staying in your room all the time—they want to know what you're *doing*. [P. 118]

This passage is clearly a parallel to the Pirandellian escape into artistic form, the same desire that from time to time marks Rosencrantz and Guildenstern and also Gladys. Ironically, both John Brown and Gladys speak of their retreat in terms of clean linen. Brown, too, seeks to be free of the fundamental human responsibilities of acting and thinking. He wishes to be directed, to find permanence against the mutability of human existence. "I came for the white calm, meals on trays and quiet efficiency, time passing and bringing nothing" (p. 120). he tells nurse Maggie Coates, his confidante.

The world outside the hospital from which Brown seeks haven is subtly presented through a series of brief scenes in which the hospital's chief doctor attempts to find an excuse for removing Brown. First he tries the police, then he investigates the records of a psychiatrist friend, finally he resorts to checking fingerprint units. Meanwhile, the routinized society within the hospital tries to interest Brown in some therapeutic work, but he participates only after they make the decision as to what specific tasks he should fulfill. He agrees to paint when the matron assigns him a subject, an English countryside. In other words, Brown is content to reduce himself to an absolutely passive being.

The pathetic nature of Brown's retreat is made clear in two passages. In the first he describes the safety of the hospital atmosphere:

> Fire, flood and misery of all kinds, across the world or over the hill, it can all go on, but this is a private ward; I'm paying for it. . . .I mean, a hospital can carry on, set loose from the world. . . . . You need never know anything, it doesn't touch you.[Pp. 128–129]

In the other he recalls the other time in his life when he was happy—as a prisoner during the war:

> The war was going on but I wasn't going to it any more. They gave us food, life was regulated, in a box of earth and wire and sky, and sometimes you'd hear an aeroplane miles up, but it couldn't touch you. [P. 132]

A further parallel may be drawn between Brown and Gladys. She had ambitions to be a nun but was rejected for her unwillingness to believe. Brown has that same kind of dream:

> Then I thought I'd be a sort of monk, but they wouldn't have me

because I didn't believe, didn't believe enough for their purposes. I asked them to let me stay without being a proper monk but they weren't having any of that . . . .What I need is a sort of monastery for agnostics. [P. 134]

Both Gladys and Brown are unable to sustain belief in a supernatural being who controls world order. However, they differ in that Gladys is not content to remain insulated within herself. She has established a relationship with Frank and dreams of escaping her plight. Brown, on the other hand, is quite content to stand aside from the roll of time and to observe the world dispassionately. In sum, he senses no absurdity on the personal level, the level that traditionally haunts absurdist figures. Rather, he is frightened only by outside society.

Eventually Brown is removed from the hospital. As the Doctor insists, he must "connect." He must confront society and become a part of it. This play is the first of Stoppard's in which the primary responsibility of the main character is to society itself. In that respect, it serves as a prelude to Stoppard's two most recent full-length plays, *Jumpers* and *Travesties*, which will be discussed more fully in the next chapter.

Albert's Bridge (1967)

The development from Gladys to John Brown to the title character of *Albert's Bridge* is clear. Gladys works at a job which alerts her to the absurdity of the world, and that knowledge destroys her. Brown is cognizant of the absurdity, and so as to avoid confrontation he seeks retreat and a form of living death. Albert recognizes the absurdity but hopes to surmount it by withdrawing into an unsullied private world.

Albert's Bridge, originally written for radio and awarded the *Prix Italia* in 1968, has also been produced on stage. However, again one must wonder if the great chaos of life is not better left to the infinite range of the listener's imagination rather than limited by production in miniature on stage.

The initial conflict of the play is established in the opening scene, when four men are painting a bridge. All but Albert are unhappy at their work, and their point of view is expressed by Dad: "I've spread my life over those girders, and in five minutes I could scrape down to my prime."[8] To him the bridge epitomizes the tedium and meaninglessness of life. But for Albert the task holds great meaning:

> Simplicity—so. . .contained; neat; your bargain with the world, your wages, your time, your energy, your property, everything you took out and everything you put in, the bargain that has carried you this far—all contained there in ten layers of paint, accounted for. Now that's something; to keep track of everything you put into the kitty, to have it lie there, under your eye, fixed and immediate—there are no consequences to a coat of paint. [P. 9]

As Albert grows more and more absorbed with his work (a variety of the Pirandellian escape into form), he gradually assumes the stature of a Sisyphus, as he contemplates the absurdity of modern life from his perch on the bridge tower. He turns away from his youth and education, for although he has extensive undergraduate training in philosophy and once was safely headed toward a career in academe, the potential complications of that career seem unnecessarily intrusive when compared to the tranquility he has discovered:

> It reduced philosophy and everything else. I got a perspective. Because that bridge was—separate—complete—removed, defined by principles of engineering . . .the whole thing utterly fixed by rules that make it stay up. It's complete, and a man can give his life to its maintenance, a very fine bargain. [Pp. 15–16]

Slowly this admiration turns into an affection and finally into an obsession that transcends all personal relationships: those with his father, mother, and wife Kate deteriorate until Albert has transferred all his love to the bridge.

The reason Albert is so able to devote himself is the result of the efforts of the society around him, a society devoted to efficiency and devoid of feeling for individual humanity. At the beginning of the play four men are painting the bridge, a task that must be redone every two years. The invention of a new form of paint which lasts eight years stimulates the town leaders of Clufton Bay to eliminate three of the painters. This decision is reached by a series of convoluted discussions that characterize the absurd world which Stoppard traditionally depicts and from which Albert is trying to escape:

> This cycle is not a fortuitous one. It is contrived by relating the area of the surfaces to be painted—call it A—to the rate of the painting—B—and the durability of the paint—C. The resultant equation determines the variable factor X—i.e. the number of painters required to paint surfaces A at speed B within time C. For example—[P. 12]

When Albert volunteers to be that one painter, he enthusiastically praises the nature of his work:

> It's the work, the whole thing—crawling round that great basket, so high up, being responsible for so much that is so visible. Actually I don't know if that's why I like it. I like it because I was happy up there, doing something simple but so grand, without end. It doesn't get away from you. [P. 18]

He seems to echo Camus's words about Sisyphus, condemned to push the rock up the mountain forever:

> All Sisyphus' silent joy is contained therein. His rock is his thing. . . .At that subtle moment when man glances backwards over his life, Sisyphus returning toward his rock, in that slight pivoting he contemplates that series of unrelated actions which become his fate, created by him. . . .
> This universe henceforth without a master seems to him neither sterile nor futile. Each atom of that stone, each mineral flake of that night-filled mountain, in itself forms a world. The struggle itself toward the heights is enough to fill a man's heart. One must imagine Sisyphus happy.[9]

It is interesting to note that when Albert is left alone to work on the bridge Stoppard alters the language from prose to poetry, in the style of Gladys's interior monologues, thus underscoring the similarities between their roles. Both of them are at a distance from the mundane, day-to-day world. To Gladys, this knowledge is traumatic and destructive. She is crushed by the pitiable triviality of human life when it is seen from such perspective. But whereas Gladys is frightened by these implications, Albert embraces them. Indeed, he revels in them, scorning the world below in which he has no part: "I could drown them in my spit" (p. 24).

When his wife Kate speaks of their friends' taking a vacation, he is contemptuous of their weakness and need to escape work. When his own child cries, he cannot tolerate her presence. In his detachment he comes to view everything beneath his bridge as foolish and pointless. Slowly he loses feeling for all that is human. Jill Levenson compares him to the misanthropic Gulliver.[10]

This aspect of Albert's character brings a new dimension to Stoppard's work and marks a still further departure from standard absurdist drama. In plays of that tradition the daily lives of men are either ignored or disdained. They are no more than senseless bumblings, pathetic and comic. Yet in *Albert's Bridge*, and in several of Stoppard's plays to follow, we are faced with the recognition that, whatever the quality of those lives, they remain all we have. We must conduct ourselves through the maze of meetings, transactions, decisions, and piddling dilemmas that weigh us down. To retreat into artistic detachment or reclusiveness, in the manner of Albert, may be aesthetically pleasing, but to do so is damaging to one's sensibilities.

Yet at the same time we cannot deny the absurdity of our lives. From the vantage point of Gladys, Brown and Albert, and from the vantage point of the great majority of absurdist characters, life is trivial. It is valueless. In the great scheme of the universe, what is one life or one nation or even one planet? Nothing at all. And yet here we are and we must try to live and establish meaning. And yet we know that there is no meaning. And yet we must believe that there is.

This conflict is the excruciating predicament that *Albert's Bridge* suggests, one that shall be developed in Stoppard's succeeding plays. The mind is caught in a dilemma. It must feel scorn and pity at the same time and in equal proportions. To laugh too hard is to rob man of his dignity. To laugh too little is to offer man excessive dignity.

Albert's relationship with Fraser, who meets Albert on the bridge, is a telling subplot that emphasizes the nature of Albert's failure. Fraser's fears are much like those of Mr. Moon:

> We are at the mercy of a vast complex of moving parts, any of which might fail. Civilization is in decline, and the white rhino is being wiped out for the racket in bogus aphrodisiacs. [P. 30]

He adds a bit later, "I couldn't bear the noise, and the chaos. I couldn't get free of it, the enormity of that disorder, so dependent on a chance sequence of action and reaction" (p. 31). His fears are expressed in faintly comic fashion, yet they are genuine and deserving of sympathy. One read in the pessimism of the late nineteenth century might think Fraser's apprehension is derived from a Housman poem:

> And how am I to face the odds
> Of man's bedevilment and God's?
> I, a stranger and afraid
> In a world I never made. [11]

But the vague general cry of the Shropshire poet is made specific by Fraser in a Swiftian enumeration of detail:

> Look down there. I came up because up was the only direction left. The rest has been filled up and is still filling. The city is a hold in which blind prisoners are packed wall to wall. Motorcars nose each other down every street, and they are beginning to breed, spread, they press the people to the walls by their knees, pinning them by their knees, and there's no end to it, because if you stopped making them, thousands of people would be thrown out of work. [Pp. 29–30]

Fraser is so desperate that he threatens to jump. But Albert is completely unsympathetic, going so far as to tell him, "Well, mind how you go. Don't fall" (p. 32). Albert has become so withdrawn and selfish as to be unaware of the bonds between men. He cannot "connect," as the Doctor told John Brown to do. In his attempt to become greater than a man, a figure of divine vision, Albert becomes less than a man, a figure destitute of feeling.

The dream that Albert nourishes of maintaining his private universe is shattered in two ways. First, the members of the company that sponsored his individual painting career recognize the folly of their policy and resolve to rectify the situation by having hundreds of painters finish the task in one day. At the end of the play an army of 1,800 painters marches toward a waiting Albert on the bridge, and his reaction is reminiscent of Rosencrantz and Guildenstern as they await death: "Eighteen-hundred men flung against me by a madman! Was I so important? Here they come" (p. 38). Under the pressure of such weight, the bridge collapses, as Albert cries, "To go to such lengths! I didn't do them any harm! What did I have that they wanted?" (p. 39).

Just before that disaster Fraser tries to warn Albert about his second, more private, failure: "You think only of yourself—you see yourself as the centre, whereas I know that I am not placed at all—" (p. 37). Clearly, as Levenson points out about the bridge, "the principles it stood for, the solace it gave, are ultimately as illusory and destructible as the logic that governs the world beneath."[12] The final truth of *Albert's Bridge* is thus one rare in absurdist drama: an assertion of the essential unity among men.

The Real Inspector Hound (1968)

In the opening tableau of *The Real Inspector Hound* can be seen the conflict that will dominate the play: a conflict between the nature of role playing and the power of the individual to shape one's own destiny. The tableau is of the audience facing what seems to be a mirror image of itself. That image turns out to be but a picture. However, the impression has been made, and the audience is left with the sensation of role uncertainty, a feeling that permeates all aspects of the succeeding drama.

The two figures who occupy the seats remaining visible are drama critics named Moon and Birdboot. Moon is on stage as the curtain rises, and his name is one familiar from other Stoppard works. More important, his character is similar to a host of other Stoppard figures in that his chief purpose in life is self-definition. A second-string critic, his societal role supersedes his personal worth. It matters not who he is, but what he is:

> It is as if we only existed one at a time, combining to achieve continuity. I keep space warm for Higgs. My presence defines his absence, his absence confirms my presence, his presence precludes mine.[13]

At the end of *Rosencrantz and Guildenstern Are Dead* Guildenstern reflects, "Death is not anything. . . . death is not . . . It's the absence of presence, nothing more . . . the endless time of never coming back" (p. 124). Moon senses that when he is not serving as fill-in for the chief critic Higgs, he is, in society's terms, dead. Therefore, like Mr. Moon, like Gladys, like John Brown, and like Albert, he views his life as rather contemptible, mostly useless, and utterly meaningless. And like every one of those characters, he is attempting to formulate a life pattern that will engender dignity in his existence. His desperation is summed up by his tirade of imagined revolution, when all second-stringers and assistants rise up to slaughter their superiors (p. 10). Perhaps the significance of his name, in this play and in other Stoppard works, might be considered at this point. "Moon" implies a touch of madness but also the image of one body in space floating around another, more significant body. And that is just what Moon is, a second-stringer floating about a world that regards him as a minor appendage.

Birdboot, whose name suggests the ultimate triviality, is quite properly the opposite of Moon. He is decidedly content with life, a sensualist in the tradition of Jane of *Lord Malquist and Mr. Moon*. He is plumpish, Stoppard indicates, and during the performance he daintily satisfies some of his cravings with some exotic chocolates. He also frequently indulges in affairs with actresses.

Throughout the performance Birdboot and Moon offer running commentaries on the hilariously bad play they are reviewing, a drawing room thriller, and their remarks reflect private preoccupations and desires. Birdboot's comments are directed toward the public taste, revealing his own mundane concerns: "He has created a real situation, and few will doubt his ability to resolve it with a startling dénouement. . . . For this let us give thanks, and double thanks for a good clean show without a trace of smut" (p. 42). Moon, on the other hand, probes the sheer escapist entertainment in a desperate attempt to disclose some hidden truths. He speaks of a "trichotomy of forces" (p. 31) and "the nature of identity" (p. 32). Finally the height of praise:

> I think we will find that within the austere framework of what is seen to be on one level a country-house weekend, and what a useful symbol that is, the author has given us—yes, I will go so far—he has given us the human condition— [P. 42]

He is even inspired by such "ubiquitous obliquity" (p. 42) to recall a dozen literary names, climaxing with Dorothy L. Sayers. Birdboot concludes simply, "A rattling good evening out. I was held" (p. 43).

The play that they are watching is a most conventional, although totally inept, production. Its primary tension emerges from the knowledge that an escaped madman, who may have appeared on stage under the name of Simon Gascoyne, is loose in the vicinity of isolated Muldoon Manor. The atmosphere of mystery is created by police messages such as "Essex County police are still searching in vain for the madman who is at large in the deadly marshes of the coastal region. . . . Meanwhile police and volunteers are combing the swamps with loud-hailers, shouting, "Don't be a madman, give yourself up" (pp. 19–20).

Although on the surface the play-within-the-play is just a compendium of theatrical clichés spiced with a bit of nonsense, it does, in fact, follow through the central image of the play established by the opening mirror scene: that of action on the stage reflecting the life of the audience and, consequently, of the outside world. For instance, the central theme of this mock-thriller is a threatening sense of madness. Potential destruction of unknown origin lurks outside. Furthermore, the reaction inside Muldoon Manor is in the spirit of a game. Depthless, emotionless characters flit back and forth across the stage without purpose or serious motivation. The dialogue is filled with the patterns of meaningless vaudevillian cross talk. The wheelchair-confined Lord Magnus nearly runs over Simon with the following dialogue:

MAGNUS: How long have you been a pedestrian?
SIMON: Ever since I could walk. [P. 26]

In a later moment of crisis, Inspector Hound, who is conducting the search for the escaped madman, panics:

HOUND (*snatching the phone*): I'll call the police!
CYNTHIA: But you are the police!
HOUND: Thank God I'm here— [P. 40]

Such exchanges contribute to an atmosphere of irrationality and mindless movement. But more telling is the gradual synchronization between the offstage characters. At first, Moon still ponders his relationship with Higgs and the third-string critic Puckeridge, while Birdboot becomes absorbed in the action of the play:

> MOON: Higgs never gives me a second thought. I can tell by the way he nods.
> BIRDBOOT: Revenge, of course.
> MOON: What?
> BIRDBOOT: Jealousy.
> MOON: Nonsense—there's nothing *personal* in it—
> BIRDBOOT: The paranoid grudge— [P. 20]

As the play progresses, however, the intermingling grows more suggestive, as Birdboot, who had earlier confessed preference for the actress playing Felicity, suddenly expresses his admiration for the woman playing the role of Cynthia. And the implications of his infatuation become more unnerving.

For instance, before the play-within-the-play begins, Moon hints to Birdboot about certain rumors concerning Birdboot's extra-marital affairs. The latter's reaction is one of outrage:

> How dare you. Don't you come here with your slimy insinuations! My wife Myrtle understands perfectly well that a man of my critical standing is obliged occasionally to mingle with the world of the footlights, simply by way of keeping *au fait* with the latest— . . .
>
> That a critic of my scrupulous integrity should be vilified and pilloried in the stocks of common gossip—[P. 13]

Such recitations have a theatrical flair that render them somewhat overdone, an impression reinforced when Moon points out the actress with whom Birdboot was seen the previous evening. Birdboot responds:

> Are you suggesting that a man of my scrupulous integrity would trade his pen for a mess of pottage? Simply because in the course of my profession I happen to have struck up an acquaintance—to have, that is, a warm regard, if you like, for a fellow toiler in the vineyard of greasepaint—I find it simply intolerable to be pillified and viloried—[P. 23]

The exaggerated language and imagery suggest a rehearsed monologue dredged up to cover his guilt. In short, he is playing a role in life, and his language reflects as much.

Thus three dramas are established. The first is the play-within-the-play that all are observing. The second is Moon's relationship with Higgs and Puckeridge, the role he is playing in relation to them. The third is Birdboot's offstage philandering and the transfer of his affections from one actress to another. What remains for Stoppard to do is show how these dramas are, at their core, similar.

Therefore they slowly blend together. At the end of its second act, the play-within is focused on twin questions of murder plots and jilted lovers, and the following lines are uttered by the observing critics, with Moon reflecting on Higgs and Birdboot reflecting on the actress playing Cynthia:

MOON: Yes, getting away with murder must be quite easy pro-
            vided that one's motive is sufficiently inscrutable.
BIRDBOOT: Fickle young pup! He was deceiving her right, left
            and centre.
MOON (*thoughtfully*): Of course, I'd still have Puckeridge be-
            hind *me*. . . .
BIRDBOOT: She needs someone steadier, more mature. . . .
MOON: . . .And if I could, so could he. . . .
BIRDBOOT: Yes, I know this rather nice hotel, very discreet,
            run by a man of the world. . . .
MOON: Uneasy lies the head that wears the crown.
BIRDBOOT: Breakfast served in one's room and no questions
            asked.
MOON: Does Puckeridge dream of me? [P. 41]

The plot onstage is becoming unified with the two plottings offstage. Of course, this dramatic technique is not unfamiliar. What Stoppard does next, however, is literally to bring the three plots together, and here his achievement is special. At the beginning of Act 3 of the thriller, the phone rings, but none of the play's characters is on stage to answer it. Moon, for some reason, is moved to pick up the phone, and the caller turns out to be Birdboot's wife, to whose love Birdboot has previously expressed undying fidelity. Moon turns the phone over to Birdboot, who apologizes to his wife Myrtle for any indiscretion. But before he can retake his seat, Felicity arrives and speaks to him of the previous evening when they had been out together. From this point on, madness rules. Birdboot is somehow pressed into playing Simon, fending off accusations in the play with defenses of his offstage actions. A dead body, which has been lying onstage since the beginning of the play, is discovered by Moon to be Higgs, the first-string critic. Suddenly Moon becomes part of the action, for Birdboot is somehow shot dead, and Moon becomes Inspector Hound. The complications and levels of reality pile insanely on top of one another, until Moon is shot by another character who turns out to be Puckeridge.

The impact of this climactic series of events is the reduction of the offstage roles of Moon and Birdboot, and by implication the reduction of all offstage life, to a charade. All action is equally meaningless. It is tempting in analyzing this play to limit those reflections on life's triviality to the critics alone, under the assumption that Stoppard, a former drama critic himself, is merely having some fun at the expense of his former professsion. And surely the play does contain marvelous parodies of critical jargon and catchphrases and of theatrical criticism in its lordly detachment and superiority. Yet to so limit the scope of Moon and Birdboot is to miss the implications of their roles.

Irving Wardle has written of Stoppard's plays, "His work is a series of looking-glass adventures, with the difference that his mirrors reflect nothing but themselves. There is no starting point in actuality."[14] This evaluation is particularly appropriate to *The Real Inspector Hound*, for here Stoppard seems without doubt to be depicting a world of artificiality, where masks substitute for reality while the inner man lies hidden.

In this respect *The Real Inspector Hound* is an inverse of Pirandello's dramatization of the question of art versus reality. In *Six Characters in Search of an Author* the characters are invested with the same dignity, perhaps even a greater dignity, than the actors. The drama becomes as important as life, as tragic and noble and deserving of respect. In Stoppard's play the drama is intended to reflect the unimportance of life, as both art and life are turned into absurd enterprises.

Like Rosencrantz and Guildenstern, Moon and Birdboot are two observers who are caught up in an action that exists beyond their control, and who are likewise destroyed by it. They never quite comprehend their roles, even as they die. And despite all the parodic implications of Stoppard's play, and despite the farcical elements, the deaths of Moon and Birdboot are undeniably moving and shocking. In their position as critics, they thought themselves invulnerable, much as members of an audience feel at a performance of *The Real Inspector Hound.* The final sensation is one of nervous wonder, as those on the outside of the turmoil await the moment when they shall be drawn irrevocably into an action that destroys them.

Dirty Linen and *New-Found-Land* (1976)

Although *Dirty Linen* and *New-Found-Land* are two of Tom Stoppard's most recent plays, thematically they are closely related to *The Real Inspector Hound.* Thus they shall be discussed at this juncture.

Dirty Linen is a linguistic farce about a postulated sex scandal in the British Parliament. The setting is a meeting room for the House of Commons, where a special committee has convened to investigate various sordid rumors. The first character we meet is Maddie Gotobed, the secretary newly assigned to this committee. She enters, arranges her lingerie and other clothing, then disappears by another door. Maddie's last name is so literal in light of her soon-to-be-revealed proclivities that Stoppard seems to be recalling the theatrical world where such names were commonplace, that of Restoration Drama. The plays of that era were marked by a style and theatricality which reflected the life and values of the characters. Similarly, Stoppard is suggesting the purely theatrical lives of his characters in *Dirty Linen*. Much like Moon and Birdboot or Rosencrantz and Guildenstern, the members of Parliament soon to appear are playing a role which to a great extent determines their life patterns and individual actions.

Such a posture can be seen clearly with the entrance of Cocklebury-Smythe and McTeazle, the first two members of the committee. They are hopelessly stuffy, preoccupied with personal aggrandizement and, we soon learn, with Maddie. Their first several lines are nothing but formal phrases in Latin and French, intimating, on the one hand, a minor sophistication, but, even more important, a world of complete artificiality, where language is used to mask rather than express feeling.

In the midst of this foolishness Maddie returns, and almost immediately Stoppard invests the play with what will become a curious *leitmotif*. As Cocklebury-Smythe is ogling a pinup in the *Daily Mail* and Maddie is bending provocatively over her desk, there is a freeze and something like a flash of light on stage. Such occurrences happen intermittently throughout the play, at moments when various members of the committee become irresistibly involved with Maddie and when simultaneously she loses part of her apparel. One must be careful about reading too deeply into a play so firmly rooted in the pure-farce tradition, but almost certainly such moments, which Stoppard indicates in the text with the exclamation "Strewth!", must be taken to represent the theatrical nature of the world he is depicting. It is a charade, a put-on, a gesture without substance.

As the other members of the committee enter at various moments, it becomes apparent that all of them have had affairs with Maddie and that she is the "mystery woman" they are to be investigating. Drawers and various undergarments appear from satchels at awkward moments and are passed around, sat on, and tossed aside with breathtaking speed. Yet always the parliamentarians struggle hilariously to maintain their dignity, using their linguistic skills to disguise their true feelings. For instance, soon after Maddie returns to the meeting, Cocklebury-Smythe and McTeazle try to warn her about saying anything that might reveal their relationships. Thus, while seeming to instruct her about the nature of a quorum in each other's presence, they are sneaking words to Maddie:

> COCKLEBURY-SMYTHE: Are we going to have a quorum? You may not be familiar with the term quorum incidentally *if anyone asks you where you had dinner last night* it's a Latin word meaning 'of which or of whom.' [15]
> McTEAZLE: Quite simply, it's the smallest number of members of a committee necessary to constitute said committee, for example, say you were *nowhere near the Coq d'Or on Saturday night* then the smallest number of members without which a quorum can't be said to be a quorum—[P. 21]

Perhaps the outstanding characteristic of this play is the verbal fireworks that Stoppard creates. Always the conversations with Maddie are tinged with *double entendre*:

> McTEAZLE: I can see, Miss Gotobed, that there is more to you than your name suggests—by which I mean (*trying to accelerate out of trouble*) that you don't spend all your time flat on your back—or your front—your side, flat on your side, sleeping, fast asleep, when you could be doing your homework instead of living up to your name, which you don't, that's my point. [Pp. 21–22]

The humor is all the stronger as we see a politician, for

whom language is usually a defense mechanism, now becoming the victim of language which forces him to reveal that which he seeks to hide. Of course, Stoppard also indulges in his favorite pastime, nonsense lines:

> WITHENSHAW: I can see you know your way around these committees, Miss Gotobed. You do speedwriting, I suppose?
> MADDIE: Yes, if I'm given enough time. [P. 29]

As Withenshaw, the chairman, sneaks some floating underwear back to his satchel, he catches the eye of French, the most sanctimonious member of the committee, who asks:

> FRENCH: What is *that*?
> WITHENSHAW: Pair of briefs.
> FRENCH: What are they doing there?
> WITHENSHAW: It's a brief case. [P. 43]

And Withenshaw then moves the conversation to other matters.

Much as in *The Real Inspector Hound*, complications, both linguistic and circumstantial, pile up insanely in this play. The primary issue is how detailed a report the committee should release. It is ultimately Maddie's decision, spoken through the other characters, that they dispense with a detailed study that might well involve them all in a public scandal and instead offer a statement indicating:

> FRENCH: That it is the just and proper expectation of every Member of Parliament, no less than for every citizen of this country, that what they choose to do in their own time and with whom, is . . .
> MADDIE: (*prompting*): . . . between them and their conscience.
> FRENCH (*simultaneously with Maddie*): . . . conscience, provided they do not transgress the rights of others or the law of the land. [P. 72]

Maddie also seems to have been involved with virtually every name in Parliament and every newspaper editor who is mentioned. Her presence is symbolic of the great charade that is the nature of political institutions, and perhaps of all social institutions as well. To read too profound an interpretation or too serious a theme into this play would be inappropriate, but Maddie's last line, and the last line of the play, "Finita La Commedia" (p. 73), certainly emphasizes the theatrical nature of the life here presented.

In the middle of *Dirty Linen*, the meeting adjourns, and the characters vacate the stage. Their place is taken by two other men, characters in *New-Found-Land*. One of the men, Arthur, is "a very junior Home Office Official." The other, Bernard, is "a very senior Home Office Official" (p. 54). They are convening to decide the fate of an American who had applied for British citizenship. But that question is shunted aside as the two become involved in their own reveries.

Bernard, partially deaf, partially senile, rambles on in a ridiculous story about how he won a bet from Lloyd George. The story is clearly one he has recounted hundreds of times, and it stands as perhaps the only important event in his life. He even attempts to tell it again when the other parliamentarians return. It seems to be his pleasure to slip away from reality and retreat into this story, leaving the difficulties of this world for that of his anecdote of decades before, when he was on top of life, if only for a moment. Lloyd George had foolishly believed Big Ben to be the famous clock, not the ringing bell itself. Thus Bernard won a five-pound note, which he brings forth triumphantly on all occasions.

The more extensive narrative is offered by Arthur, who, at Bernard's mention of America, launches into an extensive monologue expounding his views of that land. It is a compilation of tourist posters, commercials, and movie clichés about the country. He imagines himself on a cross-country train ride, meeting the glories of the land one by one:

The train drives relentlessly on, dividing whiteframe villages from their churches, and children from their hoops. And the woods give way to suburbs, to stockyards and slaughter houses, and the wind is slamming off the Great Lake as we pull round the Loop into Chicago—Chicago!—it's a wonderful town! Tight-lipped men in tight-buttoned overcoats and grey fedoras join the poker games. C-notes and G-notes raise the stakes. Shirt-sleeved newspapermen of the old school throw in their cards in disgust and spit tobacco juice upon the well-shined shoes of anyone reading a New York paper. A cheerful shoeshine boy with a flashing smile catches nickles and dimes as he crouches about his business. [P. 62]

Arthur's monologue parallels Bernard's story. Both speeches are retreats into an illusionary world. And both men live an existence of theatrics.

Here is where *New-Found-Land* joins with *Dirty Linen* and other Stoppard plays. When these two committeemen are forced to work on the application, brief though that work is, they cannot communicate, and their reality is uncomfortable. It is when they escape into their make-believe visions that they are content. Even in this brief playlet Stoppard again develops one of his important themes: theatrical form as respite from the pressures of daily existence.

After Magritte (1970)

The title "After Magritte" suggests the inventive works of the artist René Magritte (1898–1967), who might be considered the quintessential surrealist painter. This one-act play stands somewhat outside the mainstream of Stoppard's writing, but, despite its unusual features, it does share some familiar Stoppard strategies and implications.

To appreciate this play one must understand the basic feature of Magritte's paintings and of surrealist art in general. The fundamental concept underlying surrealism is the unification of opposites:

This drive is a constant and applies to all the various dichotomies of the surrealist world view: the idea and the concrete, the eternal and the immediate, the universe and the individual. In each case the two extremes must be reconciled in order for either one to fulfill, however briefly, its own nature. . . .

The tension inherent in the willed unification of opposites which are straining apart lent a kind of quivering energy to all the movement's activities. [16]

The drive for unity, which André Breton in *Nadja* termed "convulsive beauty," became the hallmark of the surrealist movement. And as a source of such images they looked to dreams, a sphere beyond the control of education, societal custom, and other sins of rationality and intellect. Breton sought to liberate art through the technique of "automatic writing," the act of creating without any preconceived notions of subject and form and without the critical constraints of reason. The product is a free transmission of the unconscious, which is thereby turned into a revelatory instrument which sees no barriers between forms of life. The world of the unconscious thus represents a bottomless well of metaphor and imagery yielding the essential unity of the universe, the essential identity of all life.

The result of such theory in painting is the creation of virtually new objects. Natural laws are dismissed, and all the traditional properties that objects hold are eliminated, as two or more "objects intermingle in an atmosphere all their own, governed by new laws of perspective, and against a new visual horizon." [17]

One Magritte painting that exemplifies such theory is "Le Modèle Rouge," an object which at its top has properties of a boot and at bottom has properties of a human foot. The result is a new creation with entirely new properties, and the viewer's perspective must change, as he or she tries to come to grips with a new reality.

It is in such a state of uncertainty that Stoppard places the characters in this play. The opening scene of *After Magritte*, however, suggests more the purely nonsense tradition of N. F. Simpson than that of surrealism. The characters on stage are the mother, reposing on an ironing board, with one foot against the iron; Thelma, dressed to go out dancing; and Reginald, standing on a chair, half-dressed, next to a lamp shade hanging from the ceiling. Behind them a policeman gazes through the window. The crux of the plot is that on the way home that afternoon from an exhibition of Magritte's paintings the three passed a man who may have committed a crime. Just who he was, what he was wearing, and the very nature of his identity are less certain, and the remainder of the play is devoted to answering those questions.

The significance of the title, then, is twofold. First, it could be taken to mean "after seeing Magritte," and after looking at the world through surrealist eyes. The more plausible interpretation is "in the style of Magritte." The opening tableau described above remains by direction frozen for a few moments, as though it were a painting. And the positions of the characters and objects have no apparent logic to them, again much in the style of a surrealist painting.

Furthermore, the object of concern, that passing figure, is equally bizarre. Thelma imagines him to have been a one-legged football player, clad in a striped uniform, wearing a white beard, and carrying a football under his arm. Reginald insists that the figure was an old man wearing his pajamas, with a face covered with shaving cream, and carrying a tortoise. The uncertainty is characteristic of surrealist art, which is founded on perception of the unfamiliar and the irrational.

In addition, the dialogue throughout the play is fraught with nonsense lines:

THELMA: My legs are insured for £5,000!
HARRIS: Only against theft![18]

And when a Scotland Yard investigator appears:

FOOT: I am Chief Inspector Foot.
HARRIS: Not Foot of the Y— [Pp. 25–26]

The ridiculous is accepted as calmly as the commonplace. Thelma and Reginald forget whose mother is staying with them. Mother's foot lies against the iron until suddenly she yowls in pain. The family attends the Magritte festival only because of Mother's devotion to the tuba. Eager to explore every reference to her instrument and hearing that a tuba figures in one of Magritte's paintings, she insists on attending the exhibit.

Such nonsense elements abound, quite appropriate in a work about surrealism, a movement dedicated to tearing down the walls of logic and rationality. Were this play directly in the surrealist tradition, Stoppard would have the confusions stand unexplained. For inherent in the nature of pure surrealism is that a work of art should never explain itself, nor should a reasoning process even cause its creation. And if this play were the product of such technique, all the contradictions and uncertainties would be purely arbitrary and consequently unresolvable.

But such is not Stoppard's approach either to the theater or to the world by 1970. The one-legged witness is revealed to be Inspector Foot himself, and all other questions are answered. In this respect, the play is more clearly related to Stoppard's other writings than to surrealism. He is not content to leave the audience suspended in limbo, in a world devoid of reason. Rather, he makes all the disparate elements seem rational—once again demonstrating his commitment against man's retreat into solitude in an effort to counteract absurdity, and insisting on man's confrontation with absurdity.

Where Are They Now (1970)

Where Are They Now is a realistic radio play which explores one aspect of Stoppard's absurdist writing: the reliance on memory and illusions of the past to sustain us. The setting is a reunion dinner for some old boys of a British public school, and the plot moves back and forth between the school days of 1945 and the present memory of them in 1969.

The crux of the drama rests in the nature of the past and man's natural distortion of it. The graduates returning for their yearly dinner speak of their schoolboy days with a roughshod affection, recalling their miseries with good-humored nostalgia. For instance, the French teacher named Jenkins who used to beat them with a stick and otherwise terrify them now earns some rugged praise and the compliment: "Never did us any harm—a few thumps with the end of a rope to keep us up to scratch. No good sending a bunch of ninnies into the world, what say you, Gale?" [19]

It is Gale who attempts to shock the celebrants into reality. When news of Jenkins's death is learned during the dinner, Gale refuses to rise in his honor: "We walked into French like condemned men. We were too afraid to *learn*. All our energy went into ingratiating ourselves and deflecting his sadism to our friends" (p. 75). Gale attacks the instinctive hypocrisy of memory—the unwillingness to come to grips with the suffering and the insistence of maintaining the delusions of constant happiness.

This hypocrisy is underscored by the numerous flashbacks that accompany the dinner. In the flashbacks Dobson, the only teacher who attends, is heard as a younger man bullying his students: "Oh, don't be stupid, boy! I will not tolerate stupid replies" (p. 69). These victims turn out to be the same guests whom he now embraces as old friends: "Yes, you were an inspired lot" (p. 65). Another flashback reveals the cruel humor and pranks with which the boys tormented one another, and the return to the present makes clear that, in fact, their relationships have altered little. They still insult one another without respect for feeling. And Dobson, despite his jocular manner, still talks to them in a schoolmaster's tone, for after so many years he has been conditioned to think only on that one level: "Runcible is here—at the Headmaster's table. Do you approve of the new seating arrangements? We've always had the Old Boys' Dinner at long tables in the past, Gale, in the Chatsworth Room downstairs, but we managed to arrange a swap" (p. 68).

In addition to Gale, two other characters stand apart from this intimate group. The first is Crawford, a more recent graduate and therefore regarded by the others as an interloper. When reminded by Dobson of the unfortunate nickname he was made to bear throughout his school career, Crawford recalls a time when he savagely beat a younger student who called him that name, a boy who turns out to be the son of one of the evening's revelers. The implication is that in a few years both he and his victim will be at such a dinner, drinking toasts to one another and fabricating a more comforting version of their encounter. The cycle goes on and on.

The other character who fails to blend into the group is also named Jenkins, and his problem is that his memories do not quite match those of the others. His details are foggy, his names inaccurate. Only at the end, when he starts singing his school song, do we learn that he has been attending the wrong reunion. Perhaps his presence and ability to go un- detected so long are evidences of the similarity of all school memories and of the trials and humiliations that beset school- boys universally.

The questions that remain after the curtain falls are why the memories are so important and why the celebrants must deceive themselves about their youth. Gale, now a journalist of considerable repute, brings out this truth, reflecting on how knowledge of the triviality of it all would have helped them: "I suppose it's not very important, but at least we would have been happier children, and childhood is Last Chance Gulch for happiness. After that, you know too much" (p. 77). In this passage the relation of this play to the rest of Stoppard's work becomes evident. One hesitates to read into this realistic play too much about theatrical absurdity, but surely the fear of an unknowable, frightening world is present in Gale's tribute to his youth:

I remember once—I was seven, my first term at prep school—I remember walking down one of the corridors, trailing my finger along a raised edge along the wall, and I was suddenly totally happy, not elated or particularly pleased, or anything like that—I mean I experienced happiness as a state of being: everywhere I looked, in my mind, *nothing was wrong.* You never get that back when you grow up; it's a condition of maturity that almost *everything* is wrong, *all the time*, and happiness is a borrowed word for something else—a passing change of emphasis. [P. 77]

The same wish for retreat that has dominated so many Stoppard characters is present in Gale also. But for the first time the spokesman is not a beaten little figure, who can claim only to be a victim of the world. Rather, here we are faced with an accomplished man who can be said to have overcome the obstacles. Thus, as will be seen, *Where Are They Now* marks the beginning of the most recent phase of Stoppard's development: a commitment to those individuals who are prepared to battle the world and who are unwilling to resign themselves to solitude or complete detachment.

5/Stoppard's Later Pieces

Jumpers (1972)

In an interview in 1967, Tom Stoppard described his plans for a new play, something about a group of exiles:

> "I think this might dovetail into a thing I have about landing on the moon," he said. "You can't just land on the moon. It's much more than just a location, it's a whole heritage of associations, poetic and religious. There are probably quite a few people around who'll go mad when the first man starts chumping around this symbol in size-ten boots."[1]

Jumpers is the product of such a notion.

The opening scene of *Jumpers* is one unprecedented in Stoppard's work, and it indicates the theatrical breakthrough he is attempting here. As the curtain rises the audience is presented with no recognizable setting, not even the loneliness of that vacant Elizabethan landscape in *Rosencrantz and Guildenstern Are Dead*, but rather an empty stage with a screen as background. The first action is Dotty's entrance and her struggle to sing "Shine On, Harvest Moon." That failure is followed by the appearance of a female trapeze artist, who gradually disrobes to the approving cheers of unseen admirers. She is succeeded by a company of gymnasts, who perform a series of complicated routines. Moments later Dotty begins singing again, but she breaks down in what appears to be a mental collapse. Panic ensues until one of the gymnasts is shot. The turmoil is then cut short, as that background screen is filled with a film of some vague activity conducted by astronauts on the moon.

These events, incomprehensible for some time, are fundamental to the rest of the play. First, the song Dotty is unable to finish is a musical tribute to the moon, and her emotional instability will be understood as a reaction to the astronauts' landing there. Once an object of wonder that inspired imaginative poetry, the moon is now becoming a familiar landscape. It has been depoeticized and transformed into a cold, lifeless piece of rock.

In the middle of Act 2 Dotty explains what has happened:

> Not only are we no longer the still centre of God's universe, we're not even uniquely graced by his footprint in man's image. . . . and all our absolutes, the thou-shalts and the thou-shalt-nots that seemed to be the very condition of our existence, how did *they* look to the two moonmen with a single neck to save between them. . . . the truths that have been taken on trust, they've never had edges before, there was no vantage point to stand on and see where they stopped.[2]

This speech, perhaps the most important in the play, is a version of the crisis Stoppard has explored throughout his writing, that of man trapped in a world operating beyond his control. However, in earlier works this world is a "given," an inevitable factor in human existence, which offers no explanations about itself, how it operates, or how it has come into such a state. But Dotty's desperate cry may be understood as a personal vision, in which the state of absurdity originates from within man himself. Therefore man should not accept his existence with resignation but must assume responsibility for his acts and struggle to make his life meaningful.

Dotty admits the difficulty of maintaining respect for man in the light of the landing on the moon, which has thrust on mankind a glimpse of himself and his world in all its triviality when seen against the infinite size of the universe. Man has thus been robbed of his delusions of grandeur. He is but a miniscule creature, scurrying about aimlessly. And when people become aware of the pointlessness of their lives, lives suddenly bereft of reason and purpose, they themselves will respond by acting without reason and purpose. Thus anarchy, and absurdity, will rule.

The events on the moon that are dramatized vaguely in the

first scene and that are reported in detail immediately afterward reinforce Dotty's fears. The two astronauts discovered "that the damage on impact had severely reduced the thrust of the rockets that are fired for take-off. Millions of viewers saw the two astronauts struggling at the foot of the ladder until Oates was knocked to the ground by his commanding officer" (p. 23). In other words, the survival instinct takes control over man. His capacity for violence and destruction is not limited to the earth and its artificial social structures. And once the imposed restraints of law are lifted, as on the moon, man will revert to his primitive instincts and dispense with his humanity.

The group which seems to embody those instincts is the gymnasts of the first scene, who turn out to be members of the Radical-Liberal Party, celebrating their seizure of the British government. Their specific process of gaining power is never established, but as Dotty remarks, "It's not the voting that's democracy, it's the counting" (p. 35).

Before we learn the precise nature of the Radical-Liberals, the impression they offer is that they are the manifestation of the absurd world Stoppard establishes in all his works. The Gymnasts, one small segment of the Radical-Liberals, are apparently irrational, wandering intermittently about the stage performing disorganized gyrations. We learn that one member, Sam Clegthorpe, their spokesman for agriculture and an acknowledged agnostic, has been named Archbishop of Canterbury. And their leader, Sir Archibald Jumper, is "a doctor of medicine, philosophy, literature, and law, with diplomas in psychological medicine and P. T. including gym" (p. 61).

The other character who echoes Stoppard's earlier works is Dotty herself, a figure very much like Jane in *Lord Malquist and Mr. Moon*. Dotty, too, is a devotee of her own body, and her bedroom is likewise the scene of numerous affairs. The parallel grows more significant when the body of the dead gymnast, shot in the opening scene, remains in her closet throughout the first act, much as Marie's body lies in Jane's house in the novel.

However, whereas Jane functions under the guise of perfect health and happiness, Dotty confesses her own misery. She has retired from the stage, and her panic at man's landing on the moon has resulted in an emotional collapse. She mopes about her room, wailing. She carries on an affair with Archie Jumper, flaunting his presence in the face of George. She is photographed in the nude. She seduces police Inspector Bones, who has come to investigate the murder of the gymnast. She now seeks to be a creature of instinct, like Jane, using such activity as a recourse against the absurd world she envisions around her.

Standing in rational opposition to such a view of the world is her husband George Moore, whom we meet in the middle of the opening scene, the celebration of the Radical-Liberal victory. If Dotty represents the body, George is the representation of the mind. He is a professor of philosophy, in the tradition of the real-life philosopher G. E. Moore. And throughout the play, as he is ruminating in philosophical fashion preparing for an annual university debate, he is constantly interrupted by Dotty's cries for help. In the first scene she shouts about "Wolves" and "Rape" and "Murder," to which George only responds: "Dorothy, I will not have my work interrupted by these gratuitous acts of lupine delinquency" (p. 26).

Clearly, George falls in the tradition of Stoppard's protagonists, those figures befuddled by the world and seeking some manner of counteracting its absurdity. His most important predecessor in Stoppard's work is probably Mr. Moon, who sought order through historical study and literary discipline. George attempts to formulate order out of chaos through philosophical inquiry.

Much of George's ruminating is effective parody of philosophical thinking. The contemporary British philosopher A. J. Ayer has commented that the author's characterization is exceedingly funny and even affectionate.[3] He even adds, "This is very fine parody, and like all the best parodies could quite often be mistaken for the original."[4] For example,

To ask "Is God?" appears to presuppose a Being who perhaps isn't . . . and thus is open to the same objection as the question, "Does God exist?" . . . but until the difficulty is pointed out it does not have the same propensity to confuse language with meaning and to conjure up a God who may have any number of predicates including omniscience, perfection and four-wheel-drive but not, as it happens, existence. [P. 24]

When these characters such as Dotty, George, and the Jumpers are considered together, they seem perfectly suited to a standard absurd play and, in particular, a play by Stoppard. And when we consider, in addition, the dramatic structure of *Jumpers*, that impression is reinforced. The play is largely without plot, exposition, development, and denouement. Rather it is a synchronization of events that deal with a certain group of characters. To insist on a more detailed organization would be inaccurate. Thus *Jumpers* seems to have all the characteristics of absurd drama, with the special addition that Stoppard has concretized his absurd world in the form of a university philosophy department.

Furthermore, were George's philosophical passages no more than parody, meaningless clusters of words unable to rise above the level of nonsense, the play would fit even more nicely into the absurdist format, in which rationality and communication are impossible. George's attempts at understanding his world would leave him nowhere, or at least in no better a situation than at the beginning of the play.

But such is not the case. Stoppard here is moving beyond that absurdist void, and George's extended disquisitions are a positive step out of the disjointed world of playwrights such as Beckett and Ionesco. His philosophical speeches are not simple parody; they are to be taken seriously and not just in relation to the academic and philosophical worlds. These speeches must be examined as reflective of society at large and as part of man's own contribution to the state of absurdity within which he exists.

A. J. Ayer has described the play as one with a central argument:

The argument is between those who believe in absolute values, for which they seek a religious sanction, and those, more frequently to be found among contemporary philosophers, who are subjectivists or relativists in morals, utilitarians in politics, and atheists or at least agnostics.[5]

The specific philosophical problem at the basis of George's inquiry is whether moral judgments are absolute or relative, whether their truth lies in correspondence with the facts of the world or whether they are merely personal expressions of emotion. Spokesmen for the two primary schools of thought on this issue have been G. E. Moore and A. J. Ayer.

According to Moore, goodness is an actual property possessed by things in the world. Thus if we affirm that some object is good and if, in fact, the object possesses the property of goodness, then our judgment is actually true. If we affirm that some object is good and the object does not possess the property of goodness, then our judgment is actually false. How is it known whether an object possesses the property of goodness? According to Moore, often referred to as an "ethical intuitionist," moral truths can be known to be true "by intuition," which is to say that their goodness is self-evident. In his book *Principia Ethica* Moore writes:

Whenever he thinks of 'intrinsic value,' or 'intrinsic worth,' or says that a thing 'ought to exist,' he has before his mind the unique object—the unique property of things—which I mean by 'good.'[6]

The opposing viewpoint has been defended by Ayer, who has argued that ethical judgments are no more than expressions of emotion:

Thus if I say to someone, "You acted wrongly in stealing that money," I am not stating anything more than if I had simply said "You stole that money." In adding that this action is wrong I am not making any further statement about it. I am simply evincing my moral disapproval of it. It is as if I had said, "You stole that money," in a peculiar tone of horror, or written it with the addition

of some special exclamation marks. The tone, or the exclamation
marks, adds nothing to the literal meaning of the sentence. It
merely serves to show that the expression of it is attended by
certain feelings in the speaker.[7]

The crucial aspect to this viewpoint is that, contrary to Moore's
position, ethical judgments do not correspond to any facts of
the world; they cannot be false or true. They are merely expressions of feeling, indicating one's own personal reaction to
things in the world.

Stoppard's George Moore clearly represents the position of
the philosopher G. E. Moore. George even goes so far as to
indicate his plans "to set British moral philosophy back forty
years, which is roughly when it went off the rails" (p. 46). A.
J. Ayer's *Language, Truth, and Logic* was published in 1936,
so George's target is obvious. Perhaps the most important statement of George's philosophical commitment takes place in
Act 2:

> But when we say that the Good Samaritan acted well, we are
> surely expressing more than a circular prejudice about behaviour.
> We mean that he acted kindly—selflessly—*well.* And what is our
> approval of kindness based on if not on the intuition that kindness
> is simply good in itself and cruelty is not. [P. 66]

Several characters, on the other hand, support the ethical
position defended by Ayer, that known as "emotivism." Dotty,
for instance, remarks, quoting Archie Jumper, "Things and
actions, you understand, can have any number of real and veri-
fiable properties. But good and bad, better and worse, these
are not real properties of things, they are just expressions of our
feelings about them" (p. 41).

But the opponent who occupies George's thoughts for most
of the play is Professor of Logic Duncan McFee, George's
opponent in the upcoming annual debate on the topic of
"Man—good, bad or indifferent." McFee is the assassinated
gymnast, one learns later, but his philosophical statements,

which approximate the ideas of Ayer, are the ones George works hardest to counteract.

The essential predicament which confronts George is made clear at the beginning of a dictation to his secretary, when, reflecting on the nature of God, he comments, "There is presumably a calendar date—*a moment*—when the onus of proof passed from the atheist to the believer, when, quite suddenly, secretly, the noes had it" (p. 25). With some desperation he consistently tries to affirm belief in God, but he always concludes by relying on the first-cause argument, which, as Ayer explains, "is notoriously fallacious, since it starts from the assumption that everything must have a cause and ends with something that lacks one."[8] By the end of the play George is still insisting, though he has been unable to formulate specific proof:

> I don't claim to *know* that God exists, I only claim that he does without my knowing it, and while I claim as much I do not claim to know as much; indeed I cannot know and God knows I cannot. [P. 71]

Again he must resort to "intuition." Something innate within him tells him God exists, and that is what he believes.

Ultimately all George's beliefs rest on a faith that cannot be proven. He relies on something indefinable within him that makes him human, that offers him values of ethical, religious, and aesthetic order.

Despite the nobility of George's intentions, he is, like all of Stoppard's protagonists, from time to time a comic figure. He is described as the classic caricature of a professor: "flannels and shabby smoking jacket, hair awry, his expression and manner signifying remonstrance" (p. 19). But even his philosophical arguments are somewhat confused. Most apparent is his reliance on the dubious first-cause argument. In addition, he manages to confuse two of Zeno's paradoxes with a fable of Aesop. The first paradox is "Achilles and the Tortoise":

> Imagine that Achilles, the fleetest of Greek warriors, is to run a

footrace against a tortoise. It is only fair to give the tortoise a headstart. Under these circumstances, Zeno argues, Achilles can never catch up with the tortoise no matter how fast he runs . . . whenever Achilles arrives at a point where the tortoise *was*, the tortoise moves a bit ahead.[9]

The other paradox is "The Arrow":

In this paradox, Zeno argues that an arrow in flight is always at rest. At any given instant, he claims, the arrow is where it is, occupying a portion of space equal to itself. During the instant it cannot move, for that would require the instant to have parts, and an instant is by *definition* a minimal and indivisible element of time. If the arrow did move during the instant it would have to be in one place at one part of the instant and in a different place at another part of the instant.[10]

George confuses these two paradoxes with Aesop's fable about the tortoise racing the hare. He even acquires a bow and arrow and a tortoise and a hare to bring to the proposed debate, in order to demonstrate that, indeed, the hare would win the race and that the arrow would reach its target.

In Ayer's words, "What finally happens to the hare and the tortoise is the most moving moment of the play."[11] But the moment has been properly set up by the preceding action. For two acts we have seen George struggling with his own mind against impersonal philosophical and religious forces that constantly confound him. He has been deserted by his wife and hounded by Inspector Bones, who suspects him of murdering Duncan McFee. Violence has broken out on all sides. The world seems to be exploding. Throughout he has been searching for the hare, who has disappeared and to whom George has grown quite attached, bestowing on him the nickname "Thumper." And we remember that earlier in the play George fired his arrow into the air and that it disappeared over his closet.

Thus, toward the end of the play, still searching for Thumper, George notices a spot of blood on his secretary's coat and realizes it must have come from on top of the wardrobe. He reaches upward and finds Thumper impaled on the arrow. As he steps down off the chair, he crushes the pet turtle with his foot.

The impact of this moment is many-sided. The sensation is, at first, horrific at the shock of sudden death; tragic, in the light of the loss of two creatures with whom we had become so well acquainted; even comic, at George's clumsiness and helplessness as he attempts to bring order to his world. The audience scarcely knows whether to scream, cry, or laugh.

The crisis George faces is captured in the last speech of the play, offered by Archie Jumper at the symposium we have anticipated throughout. The event is presented more in the form of a trial run by a dictatorial government than as a free and open debate, and George's pleas for order and rationality are thrown aside amid songs and irrelevant questions. Finally George shouts for attention, and everyone freezes, but as he tries to articulate the values that he believes the world should hold, Jumper interrupts to insist on the values that the world does hold:

> Do not despair—many are happy much of the time; more eat than starve, more are healthy than sick, more curable than dying; not so many dying as dead; and one of the thieves was saved. . . . millions of children grow up without suffering deprivation, and millions, while deprived, grow up without suffering cruelties, and millions, while deprived and cruelly treated, none the less grow up. . . . Wham, bam, thank you, Sam. [Pp. 88–89]

The key to the speech is the last word. "Sam" refers to Samuel Beckett, and the phrase about "one of the thieves" refers, as noted above (p. 77), to a well-known statement made by Beckett:

> There is a wonderful sentence in Augustine. I wish I could remember the Latin. It is even finer in Latin than English. "Do not despair: one of the thieves was saved. Do not presume: one of the thieves was damned."

Archie's exhortation is at its core an acceptance of the state of the world, a reconciliation with the state of absurdity that Beckett had dramatized. Jumper urges us to see only the good in life, as there is little use in dwelling on the negative. His speech is a poetic, nonphilosophical version of the emotivist argument that George has been opposing throughout the play. Dramatic absurdity and philosophical argument are thus tied together, and the union reinforces the most crucial theme of the play: that mankind is not simply a passive victim in this world but can be an active participant.

On the one hand, we are presented with the philosophic thrust of the emotivists, McFee and Jumper, the view that goodness, truth, and beauty are but personal prejudices. Under such conditions man is condemned to react to stimuli, to decide which are pleasant and which are unpleasant, and to continue in the direction of the pleasant. He can ignore death, destruction, immorality. Man is thus without responsibility. He denies himself reason, sympathy, and understanding, everything that makes him human.

Stoppard, through George, is protesting such a world vision. Just as the critics' dilemma in *The Real Inspector Hound* should not be limited to members of that profession, so George's arguments should not be directed simply to members of philosophy departments, nor even just to intellectuals. Rather the play is a reaction against modern man's denial of all values and a reaffirmation of the belief that something within us makes us human, something which makes us believe in goodness and beauty. And that something must never be dismissed or forgotten.

To be sure, despite this play's intellectual interest and its place as a turning point in Stoppard's career, it is not wholly successful as drama. Harold Clurman has written, "Its point or 'thesis' is not revealed through action: it is only stated. There is no basic confrontation, conflict, or delineation of real characters."[13] The criticism is a fair one. George's long monologues, amusing and stimulating though they may be, are not dramatic. And the audience is forced to spend too much time pondering strictly academic philosophical subtleties.

Granted these limitations on the play, it nevertheless remains fascinating and important. For in this work Stoppard deals with intellectual issues, and reasoned argument is an integral component of the play. Such strategy marks a total break with absurdist writing, in which language, communication, and, consequently, rational debate have been impossible. In what stands as his boldest step in moving beyond absurdity, Stoppard dispenses with this limitation of human activity, and he begins to confront world issues directly. The difficulty of life on earth is now accepted. What matters here and in the plays to follow is how to live under those conditions.

Artist Descending a Staircase (1972)

In *Krapp's Last Tape* Beckett transformed the tape recorder into yet another actor, a manifestation of the elusive human character. In the radio play *Artist Descending a Staircase*, first broadcast 14 November 1972, Stoppard uses the tape recorder to probe the confusion that is man's memory and conscience.

The play is structured in eleven scenes, moving from the present through a series of flashbacks and then returning once again to the present. Each flashback represents episodes in the lives of three painters—their dreams and failures as well as their relationship with a blind woman who becomes mistress to one of them. Memories are set in motion by the death of one of the artists, Donner, whose demise has accidentally been recorded on tape. Each of the two survivors, Martello and Beauchamp, suspects the other of murder. But more important than this single event are the two major themes that dominate the play.

The first is one now common to Stoppard's plays: the elusive nature of truth. In the first scene Martello and Beauchamp bicker over trivial details of their life:

MARTELLO: Remember how John used to say "If Donner whistles

the opening of Beethoven's Fifth in six/eight time
once more I'll *kill him!*"?
BEAUCHAMP: John who?
MARTELLO: Augustus John.
BEAUCHAMP: No, no, it was Edith Sitwell. [14]

This is but one of many incidents in which details or names
are confused, both for comic effect and for dramatization of
the natural distortion of memory and perception.

A more important instance of distortion is the young Sophie's
attempts to remember which of three young painters she
admired. She had met them all when her eyesight was failing
but was attracted to one without knowing his name. By the
time she knew the man better, she had become blind, and the
only way she could single out her favorite was to recall him as
he was standing next to one of his paintings:

SOPHIE: It was a background of snow, I think.
DONNER: Yes, there was a snow scene. Only one.
SOPHIE: A field of snow, occupying the whole canvas—
MARTELLO: Not the whole canvas—
SOPHIE: No—there was a railing—
BEAUCHAMP: Yes, that's it—a border fence in the snow!
SOPHIE: Yes! [Pp. 40–41]

The artist turned out to be Beauchamp, with whom she went to
live. However, years later, Martello reminds Donner that the
picture Sophie described could, from another perspective,
have been Donner's: "Thick white posts, top to bottom across
the whole canvas, an inch or two apart, black in the gaps—"
(p. 52). And Donner, who of the three had been the most in love
with Sophie, realizes how his whole life was altered by Sophie's
inaccurate perceptions and memories.

The incident which best exemplifies the fallibility of human
perception and the uncertain nature of truth is the death
of Donner as recorded on the tape machine. Martello and
Beauchamp, seizing the clues, each imagine that Donner was
murdered by the other. But the audience, at the very end of the

play, realizes their mistake. What the two assumed to be Donner's snoring turns out to have been the buzzing of a fly. What they assumed to be Donner's reaction to a visiting close friend was, in fact, his triumph at locating that fly. And what they assumed to be a blow struck against Donner was his attempted swatting of the fly, and thus his subsequent fall was not a murder but an accidental death. The revelation of their ironic misconceptions comes as a shock.

These confusions are not unlike scenes from other Stoppard works. But *Artist Descending a Staircase* is built upon a second, more important, theme, and as such the play serves as another example of Stoppard's most recent phase. Once again he deals with an intellectual issue, and the question that dominates this play about artists is, naturally enough, the purpose of art. In his younger days Beauchamp is sure:

> Art consists of constant surprise. Art should never conform. Art should break its promises. . . .

> The artist is a lucky dog. That is all there is to say about him. In any community of a thousand souls there will be nine hundred doing the work, ninety doing well, nine doing good, and one lucky dog painting or writing about the other nine hundred and ninety-nine. [Pp. 42–43]

His emphasis is on freedom. The artist's goal is self-expression, without moral or political commitment. The very act of creation establishes meaning and is self-justifying.

The logical outcome of such thinking is to seek recourse in an artistic form that denies restriction, one that, according to Beauchamp,

> made anything possible and everything safe!—safe from criticism, since our art admitted no standards outside itself; safe from comparison, since it had no history; safe from evaluation, since it referred to no system of values beyond the currency it had invented. [P. 24]

In a sense, this artistic creation is as much an escape from absurdity as Albert's working on the bridge or John Brown's retreat to the hospital. Yet such exaltation of absolute artistic freedom is only a meaningless act of rebellion. Stoppard provides several examples of such efforts. Martello imagines himself working on a statue called "The Cripple," composed of a wooden man with a real leg. Beauchamp records ping-pong games, and in his older period he is reduced to collecting random sounds on his tape recorder, "the detritus of audible existence, a sort of refuse heap of sound" (p. 19). In short, Beauchamp and Martello pursue a series of artistic dead ends, work that exists only for itself and thus has no value outside itself. Donner explains the nature of their failure: "I very much enjoyed my years in that child's garden of easy victories known as the avant garde, but I am now engaged in the infinitely more difficult task of painting what the eye sees" (p. 19).

His statement may be taken as representative of the dramatic development of Stoppard through his one-act plays. It is not enough to portray an absurd world and then surrender to it through any of the dramatized methods of retreat. One must grapple with that outside world. In *Jumpers* Stoppard protests against retreat into philosophical absurdity. In *Artist Decending a Staircase* he intersplices a drama about memory and identity with some tentative questions concerning the nature of artistic enterprise. Clearly, the absurdist situations and values have become subordinate, and intellectual issues have emerged as the source of drama. In his most recent full-length play, *Travesties*, Stoppard progresses to examine more clearly the role of the artist and revolutionary in yet another step in his movement beyond absurdity.

Travesties (1974)

Historical drama is not absent from contemporary theater. Among the most notable examples are: Robert Bolt's *A Man for All Seasons* (1960), based on the life of Sir Thomas More; Peter Shaffer's *Royal Hunt of the Sun* (1964), which depicts the Spanish invasion of the Inca Empire; and Edward Bond's *Bingo* (1973), which utilizes a few facts about Shakespeare's last years to fashion a more speculative form of historical play.

In *Travesties* Tom Stoppard pursues yet another variation of historical theater, and the steps he takes are indicated by the title. No longer are titans from history set up as powerful or noble figures. Here they are reduced to a most human level, a level where they, too, are confronting the world's absurdities and struggling to counteract them.

At his starting point Stoppard uses the well-known coincidence that James Joyce, Lenin, and the Dadaist poet Tristan Tzara all happened to be at one time or another in Zurich during World War I. No historical evidence indicates that they ever encountered one another, although Tzara and his fellow Dadaists were carrying on their nightly programs of songs, poetry readings, and plays at the Cabaret Voltaire, No. 1 Spiegelgasse, directly opposite No. 6, which was inhabited by Lenin.[15] In Stoppard's imagination the three do cross paths.

But the playwright is not content just to let them meet and talk. He goes a step further, and at this point the play diverges sharply from any history play of the past. Actual historical events are not presented chronologically. Nor does one of the distinguished participants recount an orderly procession of events. Rather, Stoppard uses an historical nonentity by the name of Henry Carr, an ex-army officer who served as a minor officer in the British Consulate in Zurich during the war years. It is he who as an old man opens the play by introducing the series of encounters and in whose befuddled memory they are replayed.

The technique of dramatizing through such a frazzled mind offers many theatrical possibilities. In *Artist Decending a Staircase* Stoppard demonstrates how memory can distort the truth. In *Travesties* this phenomenon is developed to such an extent that the entire narrative structure is subject to the vagaries of memory, and the complications become bewildering.

Richard Ellman explains that the first example of such distortion is the time period itself:

> We seem to pass rapidly from 1916, when Tzara, according to his friend Hans or Jean Arp. . .gave Dadaism its title, to 1917, when Lenin, train-sealed, went to Petrograd, to 1918 and 1919, when Joyce was business manager of a company called the English Players, and quarrelled with A. Percy Bennett, the British Consul-General in Zurich and with one of his employees.[16]

Such capsulization is made apparent in the opening tableau, which takes place in the Zurich public library. At one table sits Tzara, cutting slips of paper from books and rearranging them at random, fashioning poetry, or rather antipoetry, in proper Dadaist fashion:

> Eel at enormous appletzara
> key dairy chef's hat he'lllearn oomparah!
> Ill raced alas whispers kill later nut east,
> noon avuncular ill day Clara![17]

At the next table sits Joyce, dictating the opening lines from the "Oxen of the Sun" episode of *Ulysses* to his puzzled but loyal secretary Gwendolyn:

JOYCE: Hoopsa, boyaboy, hoopsa!
GWEN: Hoopsa, boyaboy, hoopsa!
JOYCE: Hoopsa, boyaboy, hoopsa!
GWEN: Likewise thrice?
JOYCE: Uh-hum. [P. 18]

Both are indulging in a form of travesty, Tzara of the nature of art itself and Joyce of the English prose style. And as they race on, babbling in what, out of context, is but nonsense, they seem more than a little ridiculous.

At the third table sits Lenin, a more sober figure but one who is still not immune to the bizarre effects of Carr's memory. As he speaks excitedly in Russian concerning news of the

Revolution brought by his wife, Nadya, his dignity is lessened by the repeated cries of "Dah, dah" ("yes, yes"), which become inextricably tied to Tzara's shenanigans.

But the compression of time is only one part of the tricks that Carr's mind works on him. The real Carr was hired by Joyce to play Algernon in a production of *The Importance of Being Earnest* produced by Joyce. In his introduction to *Travesties* Stoppard explains that he learned the details of Carr's relationship with Joyce from Richard Ellmann's biography of Joyce.[18] Apparently Carr performed brilliantly. But Carr's personal relationship with Joyce was not cordial. Joyce paid him a fee appropriate to an amateur actor and demanded money for tickets Carr was to have sold. Carr, on the other hand, demanded payment for pants he had purchased in order to play his role and called Joyce "a cad" and "a swindler." The entire matter was taken to court in two separate trials. Joyce sued Carr for the price of his tickets, and Carr countersued for his trousers. Joyce added a second suit for libel. Joyce won the first suit, Carr the second.

But Joyce's revenge against Carr was not finished, and he bestowed on him a perverse immortality. In the "Circe" episode of *Ulysses*, the drunken soldier is named Carr. He threatens Stephen with the words, "Say, how would it be, governor, if I was to bash in your jaw?"[19] Bennett, in real life Carr's superior at the British Consulate, is turned into Carr's sergeant, although in *Ulysses* Carr is permitted to show the proper disrespect: "God fuck old Bennett! He's a white-earsed bugger. I don't give a shit for him."[20]

However, the focus of attention here must be Stoppard's Carr, through whose memory we encounter the three remarkable personalities. As the curtain rises the audience meets Carr when he is at the end of his life, chain smoking, dressed in a tattered bathrobe, and rambling on about his past and the people whom he has known. Only occasionally does he veer in the general direction of coherence. But as he himself explains, "No apologies required, constant digression being the saving grace of senile reminiscence" (p. 22). Still, Carr's rambling monologue should also be understood as Stoppard's own parody of the Joycean stream-of-consciousness. We listen to his mind run onward, as he intends to reach several conclusions. But at the end of the opening recitation he has revealed nothing except his own muddled mind and his delight with himself.

His analysis of the man Joyce, for instance, is typically chaotic:

> A prudish, prudent man, Joyce, in no way, profligate or vulgar, and yet convivial, without being spendthrift, and yet still without primness towards hard currency in all its transmutable and transferable forms and denominations . . . [P. 22]

His description of Lenin proceeds in much the same manner, saying much and telling nothing:

> As I shook the hand of this dynamic, gnomic, and yet not, I think, anaemic stranger, who with his fine head of blond hair falling over his forehead had the clean-shaven look of a Scandinavian seafaring—hello, hello, got the wrong chap, has he? [P. 23]

The last major character whom Carr introduces in his opening monologue is Tristan Tzara. This is not the first time Tzara has been mentioned in a Stoppard play. In *Artist Descending a Staircase* Donner and Beauchamp remembered the days of their youth, when they lived in Zurich and hobnobbed amid the Dadaists and other artistic revolutionaries. In their hazy memories they refer to him first as "Tarzan" and insist that, in fact, he was much too traditional an artist. They recall sitting at the Café Voltaire, with Lenin huddled nearby, and they recite a few names of those who inspired their work: Hugo Ball and Hans Arp, among others.

But the bonds between Donner and Beauchamp and Henry Carr are more than just circumstantial. Stoppard emphasizes their kinship by taking lines from *Artist Descending a Stair-*

case and transplanting them into *Travesties*. In his opening harangue Carr recalls that Tzara once "wrote his name in the snow with a walking stick and said: 'There! I think I'll call it The Alps'" (p. 25). Beauchamp, in commenting on Tzara's audacity, recalls the same incident in almost exactly the same words (p. 24). Later in the first act of *Travesties* Carr and Tzara debate the role of the artist, and in a moment of pique Carr bursts out, shouting: "What is an artist? For every thousand people there's nine hundred doing the work, ninety doing well, nine doing good, and one lucky bastard who's the artist" (p. 46). Virtually the same speech is uttered by the youthful Beauchamp in *Artist Descending a Staircase*, in defense of his own artistic autonomy (p. 43). Curiously, when in *Travesties* Tzara offers similar statements of freedom in defense of his own art, Carr strenuously opposes them.

This dichotomy of attitude about the role of the artist represents an important aspect of Stoppard's work. In the course of his plays he has moved from a passive resignation in the face of absurdity to a desire to struggle against absurdity and to move beyond it. In *Jumpers* his protagonist attempts to oppose absurdity through philosophical thought. In *Artist Descending a Staircase* Stoppard explores briefly the role of the artist against absurdity. Now, in the first act of *Travesties*, he considers the artist's role more closely.

However, before continuing this discussion, it is important to note the extent to which Carr's performance in *The Importance of Being Earnest* dictates his memories. He thinks of himself and Tzara as characters in the play, he as Algernon and Tzara as Jack, and both appear before us as two dandies right out of Wilde's play. In addition, the tone of their dialogue is pure Wilde, replete with epigrams and stylized word usage, as the world is transformed into a showcase for their own elegance:

> TZARA: But, my dear Henry, causality is no longer fashionable owing to the war.

CARR: How illogical, since the war itself had causes. I forget what they were, but it was all in the papers at the time. Something about brave little Belgium, wasn't it?

TZARA: Was it? I thought it was Serbia . . .

CARR: Brave little Serbia . . . ? No, I don't think so. The newspapers would never have risked calling the British public to arms without a proper regard for succinct alliteration.

TZARA: Oh, what nonsense you talk!

CARR: It may be nonsense, but at least it is clever nonsense.

TZARA: I am sick of cleverness. [Pp. 36–37]

These last lines are clearly adapted from Act 1 of *The Importance of Being Earnest*, when Jack concludes, "I am sick to death of cleverness."[21]

It might also be noted that early in the first act one encounters Carr's own memories of his superior Bennett, whom he reduces to the level of his own servant, a parallel to Lane in *Earnest*. Indeed, in both plays the servant is concerned with eight bottles of champagne that were consumed the previous Thursday night. And in both plays the servants' views of the world are cause for their masters' consternation. Bennett recites the propaganda of the Russian Revolution at length and in completely blank tones, and Carr finds the situation intolerable. His notion of a revolution entails "unaccompanied women smoking at the Opera" (p. 29). After enduring Bennett's diatribe, Carr resolves to keep an eye on Lenin.

These are but two of many interminglings between the plays that take place in Carr's recollections. The importance of such a theatrical strategy on Stoppard's part will be considered presently.

The conflict between Carr and Tzara is established early:

TZARA: And it is the duty of the artist to jeer and howl and belch at the delusion that infinite generations of real effects can be inferred from the gross expression of apparent cause.

CARR: It is the duty of the artist to beautify existence.

TZARA: Dada dada dada dada dada . . . [P. 37]

Tzara continues by claiming, "Nowadays, an artist is someone who makes art mean the things he does" (p. 38). Again he echoes Donner of *Artist Descending a Staircase*: "There are two ways of becoming an artist. The first way is to do the things by which is meant art. The second way is to make art mean the things you do." (p. 24).

But the conflict over art has far more extensive implications. Carr intends art to justify the essential order of the world in which he needs to believe. Tzara intends his art to mirror the essential chaos of the world, a world without reason, without order. He even insists that the World War is only "capitalism with the gloves off and many who go to war know it but they go to war because they don't want to be a hero" (p. 39). Carr strenuously resists this diminunution of his world to such a trivial level:

> I went to war because it was my *duty*, because my country needed me, and that's *patriotism*. I went to war because I believed that those boring little Belgians and incompetent Frogs had the right to be defended from German militarism, and that's *love of freedom*. *That's* how things are underneath, and I won't be told by some yellow-bellied Bolshevik that I ended up in the trenches because there's a profit in ball-bearings! [P. 40]

But Tzara refuses to accept the significance of any of it:

> You ended up in the trenches because on the 28th of June 1900 the heir to the throne of Austro-Hungary married beneath him and found that the wife he loved was never allowed to sit next to him on royal occasions. [P. 40]

Carr's only reply is to quietly chant, "We're here because we're here . . . because we're here because we're here . . . (p. 40).

It remains for Joyce at the end of Act 1 to affirm the role of the artist and, at the same time, to oppose Tzara's acceptance of absurdity. In Carr's memory Joyce is first presented as a convivial song-and-dance man, given to limericks, folk songs, and outrageous puns, who has come to Carr's home in order to enlist him to play Algernon in the production of *The Importance of Being Earnest.* Initially Carr is wary, but after learning the details of Algernon's costumes he enthusiastically accepts. While Carr and Joyce—whom Carr constantly calls "Janice" or "Doris"—retire to another room to consider the script, Tzara is left with Gwendolyn, Carr's sister in the play. Tzara entertains Gwendolyn by cutting a copy of Shakespeare's eighteenth sonnet into individual words, with the intention of rearranging them to form a work of his own creation.

But before Tzara recites his poem, Stoppard undercuts the effect by blending lines from various Shakespearean works as a substitute for Tzara's own conversation. The sequence begins after Gwendolyn recites the sonnet that Tzara is cutting into bits:

GWEN: You tear him for his bad verse? [The source is *Julius Caesar*, 3.2.34] These are but wild and whirling words, my lord. [*Hamlet*, 1.5.133]

TZARA: Ay, Madam.

GWEN: Truly I wish the gods had made thee poetical. [*As You Like It*, 3.3.16]

TZARA: I do not know what poetical is. Is it honest in word and deed? Is it a true thing? [*As You Like It*,3.3.17–18]

GWEN: Sure he that made us with such large discourse, looking before and after, gave us not *that* capability, *and* godlike reason to fust in us unused. [*Hamlet*, 4.4.36–39]

TZARA: I was not born under a rhyming planet. [*Much Ado About Nothing*, 5.2.39–40] Those fellows of infinite tongue that can rhyme themselves into ladies' favours, they do reason themselves out again. [*Henry V*, 5.2.163–65] And that would set my teeth on edge—*nothing* as much as mincing poetry. [*Henry IV*, Part 1, 3.1.133–34]

GWEN: Thy honesty and love doth mince *this matter*— [*Othello*, 2.3.247] Put your bonnet for his right use, 'tis for your head! [*Hamlet*, 5.2.96] I had rather than forty shilling my book of songs and sonnets here. [*The Merry Wives of Windsor*, 1.1.205–6]

TZARA: But since he died, and poet better prove, his for his style you'll read, mine for my—love. (Sonnet 32. 13–14) [P. 54].

He then reads his own coagulation of words, and the references among them to the weather lead Gwendolyn to quote from Wilde: "Pray don't talk to me about the weather, Mr. Tzara. Whenever people talk to me about the weather I always feel quite certain that they mean something else" (p. 55).

As Gwendolyn and Tzara, like characters from *The Importance of Being Earnest*, express their love, Joyce returns to take his hat in which Tzara had mixed up the bits of paper. Joyce leaves, only to return with the bits scattered over his clothing. Intrigued with Tzara's methods, he begins an interrogation of Tzara that parodies both the "catechism" scene in the "Ithaca" episode of *Ulysses* and Lady Bracknell's questioning of Jack in the first act of *The Importance of Being Earnest*. The tempo and intensity of the questions and replies grow more frenzied until Tzara bursts out in anger:

> Your art has failed. You've turned literature into a religion and it's as dead as all the rest, it's an overripe corpse and you're cutting fancy figures at the wake. It's too late for geniuses! Now we need vandals and desecrators, simple-minded demolition men to smash centuries of baroque subtlety, to bring down the temple, and thus, finally to reconcile the shame and the necessity of being an artist! Dada! *Dada! Dada!!* [P. 62]

And he proceeds to smash whatever crockery he can find. Joyce calmly dissects his theory:

> You are an over-excited little man, with a need for self-expression far beyond the scope of your natural gifts. . . . An artist is the magician put among men to gratify—capriciously—their urge for immortality. The temples are built and brought down around him, continuously and contiguously, from Troy to the field of Flanders. If there is any meaning of it, it is in what survives as art. . . . What now of the Trojan War if it had been passed over by the artist's touch? Dust . . . [P. 62]

Through Joyce Stoppard attempts to justify his own work, the importance of art as a counter agent to oppose the ab-

surdity of man's existence. But even Joyce admits the attempt
is only partially successful. Art does not inject meaning into
life. It simply makes the meaninglessness easier to bear by
affording us the privilege of perspective and, through the
magnification of time, bringing a new dignity to events that
otherwise pass too quickly and never receive proper attention.

One would think that Carr would be sympathetic to such
sentiments, but his own prejudices distort his appreciation.
As Joyce's speech ends, Carr slips steadily into the role of
Algernon and then reverts to the old Carr whom we met
at the beginning of the play. As Act 1 concludes, he relates
in typically bumbling fashion the details of the trials and
confesses that he imagines his own dreams of cross-examining
Joyce:

> "And what did you do in the Great War?" "I wrote *Ulysses*,"
> he said. "What did you do?"
> Bloody nerve. [P. 65]

Even in his anger he recognizes that Joyce's achievement
lifts him above the realm of common men. In acknowledging
Joyce's greatness Carr is forced to accept his own mediocrity,
and it is perhaps that awareness that frustrates him most
of all.

The second act of the play deals primarily with Lenin
and his concept of political revolution, as opposed to the
Dadaist artistic revolution and the Joycean scheme for in-
vesting man's life with dignity. Many critics have commented
upon the weakness of the early part of this act, claiming,
with some justice, that the comic spirit is diluted by the pre-
tentious polemics of Cecily's lecture on Marxism and by
Lenin's own character, which is stolid and in stark contrast
to the lighthearted spirit that characterizes Carr, Tzara,
and Joyce.

Nevertheless, Lenin is a significant figure. In the first part
of Act 2, Cecily, Lenin's assistant, promulgates his doctrine

to Carr, who is visiting her at the library. The propaganda is intertwined with dialogue and plot complications from *The Importance of Being Earnest*, as Carr's memories of the play blend bewilderingly with historical events. But Carr had another real-life role. As British Consulate he was expected to keep track of Lenin's whereabouts and to determine whether or not he should be prevented from leaving Zurich. Cecily indicates the dimension of revolution to which Lenin aspired:

> In an age when difference between prince and peasant was thought to be in the stars, Mr. Tzara, art was naturally an affirmation for the one and a consolation to the other; but we live in an age when the social order is seen to be the work of material forces and we have been given an entirely new kind of responsibility, the responsibility of changing society. [P. 74]

She continues by describing the World War as nothing but a class war. Carr responds by attacking Marx:

> [His] premise was that the people were a sensational kind of material object and would behave predictably in a material world. Marx predicted that they would behave according to their class. But they didn't. Deprived, self-interested, bitter or greedy as the case may be, they showed streaks of superior intelligence, superior strength, superior morality. . . . Legislation, unions, share capital, consumer power—in all kinds of ways and for all kinds of reasons, the classes moved closer together instead of further apart. [P. 76–77]

Such statements may be taken to represent the view of Stoppard himself. In a recent interview he commented:

> The great irony about Marx was that his impulses were deeply moral while his intellect insisted on a materialistic view of the world. His theory of capital, his theory of value, and his theory of revolution have all been refuted by modern economics and by history. . . . It was only a matter of time before somebody—it turned out to be Bernstein in 1900—somebody with the benefit of an extra fifty years' hindsight, would actually point out that Marx had got it wrong, but that it didn't matter because social justice was going to come through other means.[22]

At other points in the interview Stoppard comments on political issues directly related to *Travesties*:

> The play [*Jumpers*] reflects my belief that all political acts have a moral basis to them and are meaningless without it.
>
> I believe all political acts must be judged in moral terms, in terms of the consequences. Otherwise they are simply attempts to put the boot on some other foot. There is a sense in which contradictory political statements are restatements of each other. For instance, Leninism and Fascism are restatements of totalitarianism.
>
> The repression which for better or worse turned out to be Leninism in action after 1917 was very much worse than anything which had gone on in Tsarist Russia. . . . It is simply true that in the ten years after 1917 fifty times more people were done to death than in *fifty* years before 1917.
>
> One thing I feel sure about is that a materialistic view of history is an insult to the human race.[23]

Such sentiments are borne out ironically in the speeches of Lenin in *Travesties*. He is revealed to be not a moralist, nor even propelled by deep feelings for the downtrodden, but an egomaniac whose concept of fulfillment is his own elevation to absolute power. Tzara, on the one hand, simply equates political revolution and artistic revolution: "Artists and intellectuals will be the conscience of the revolution" (p. 83). But Lenin reveals his own aims in statements on the value of the artist:

> Today, literature must become party literature. . . . Literature must become part of the common cause of the prolateriat, a cog in the Social Democratic mechanism. . . .
> We want to establish and we shall establish a free press, free not simply from the police, but also from capital, from careerism, and what is more, *free from bourgeois anarchist individualism*. . . .
>
> Everyone is free to write and say whatever he likes, without any restrictions. But every volunteer association, including the

party, is also free to expel members who use the name of the party to advocate anti-party views. [P. 85]

While Lenin orates at the audience from a platform, Nadya, his wife, attempts to restate his words in order to soften the tone of repression and absolutism: "The *new* art seemed somehow alien and incomprehensible to him" (p. 86). Nevertheless, Lenin's own drives for personal honor and power dominate the scenes where he is at center. He even attempts to crush his own feelings for humanity for fear they will endanger his drive for power:

> But I can't listen to music often. It affects my nerves, makes me want to say nice things and pat the heads of those people who while living in this vile hell can create such beauty. Nowadays we can't pat heads or we'll get our heads bitten off. We've got to *hit* heads, hit them without mercy, though ideally we're doing violence to people. . . . Hm, one's duty is infernally hard. [P. 89]

Thus the parallels are drawn between the artistic revolutionary and the political revolutionary. In the case of both Tzara and Lenin, the act of revolution is but an extension of reveling in their own egos. Tzara judges himself the ultimate artist and the ultimate artistic authority. Lenin sets himself up as the rebel and then as ruler over all the other rebels. Each seeks to establish a private, personal tyranny.

Of the three figures who dominate this play only Joyce emerges with stature. Despite Carr's attempts to portray him as an elaborate vaudevillian, Joyce's understanding of the plight of the artist and of the artistic role among men redeems him. He holds no pretenses about changing man's condition on earth, only about alleviating some of the pain and shedding some light on the human condition through artistic creation.

In a sense, he solves Stoppard's own artistic dilemma. Throughout his work Stoppard has struggled with the question of how man can oppose absurdity. In *Travesties* he seems to have reached a reconciliation with absurdity. The human condition is immutable. To a great extent the social, political, and religious order of an individual society is irrelevant. Through art, and through the development of his own consciousness, each man must come to grips with his world. Stoppard rejects such doctrinaire panaceas as offered by Tzara and Lenin. He accepts the individual call to dignity that Joyce represents.

To be sure, Stoppard does not simply forget about the absurdist world that is so important throughout his writings. And at this point it would be useful to consider the significance of the Wilde play, scenes and dialogue of which thread through *Travesties*. The moments at which the plays intermingle are too numerous to list, but a few more instances will help elucidate Stoppard's intention.

As stated previously, in Carr's memory he is playing the role of Algernon and Tzara is playing his brother Jack. And just as Algernon is convinced in Act 1 of Wilde's play that Jack's name is actually Ernest, so Carr is convinced that Tzara's name is Tristan, despite Tzara's confusing claim that his name is Jack:

> You have always told me it was Tristan. I have introduced you to everyone as Tristan. You answer to the name of Tristan. Your notoriety at the Meierei Bar is firmly associated with the name Tristan. It is perfectly absurd saying your name isn't Tristan. [P. 45]

The speech is virtually identical to one uttered in Act 1 of *The Importance of Being Earnest*.[24]

In Act 2 of *Travesties* Carr pursues Cecily, whom he remembers working in a library. In Wilde's play she is devoted to her studying. Just as Algernon speaks of Cecily as "the prettiest girl I ever saw,"[25] so Carr speaks to Cecily in the same tone (p. 71). And the romantic confusions are resolved in the same manner:

GWEN: That's my brother.
CECILY: Your brother?
GWEN: Yes. My brother, Henry Carr.
CECILY: Do you mean that he is not Tristan Tzara the artist?
GWEN: Quite the contrary: He is the British Consul.
BENNETT: Mr. Tzara . . .
GWEN: Tristan! My Tristan!
CECILY: Comrade Jack. [Pp. 93–94]

The mixtures of dialogue and character are continuous and virtually impossible to clarify.

Such a dramatic imbroglio underscoring the debates over artistic and political revolution is reminiscent of the plight of the critics in *The Real Inspector Hound*, who are drawn into the action of the play that they are reviewing. Meanwhile, the audience grows more conscious of the artificiality of the critics' offstage lives. Similarly, those observing the action of *Travesties* come to understand all human activity as a variety of theatrical posture. Tzara, Joyce, and Lenin all may be seen as seeking the Pirandellian retreat into a role in life, one which protects them from the buffetings of absurdity. Tzara scorns all traditional art and dismisses all criticism, setting himself up as an unchallengable authority. Lenin shields himself behind the role of revolutionary, dismissing all that does not fit within his political scheme. Even Joyce retreats into the role of the artist, setting up individual standards and seeking individual achievement with little regard for the traditions of art and criticism.

Where does Carr fit into this scheme? He falls squarely into the tradition of Stoppard's protagonists, a series of inconsequential figures who are lost in the world but who attempt to formulate understanding and act accordingly. Carr retreats into his own memory and imagination, creating from the past a role for himself that offers him dignity and position. But gradually the fragility of his dream forces itself upon him. At the end of the play, once again as an old man, he speaks to the audience, but not before his wife, Cecily, naturally much older herself, insists on his telling the truth: that he hardly knew Lenin; that his relationship with Joyce was not nearly as close as he had claimed; and that Bennett, not Carr, was historically the British Consulate, and not his servant, as Carr had recalled. Carr speaks resignedly of his earlier life: "I was here. They were here. They went on. I went on. We all went on" (p. 98). His words echo the closing lines of Beckett's *The Unnameable*: "I don't know, I'll never know, in the silence you don't know, you must go on, I can't go on, I'll go on."[26] Carr's statement is recognition of the transience, the sadness, and the absurdity of life, and the need for renewed strength against such knowledge.

Yet he is not content to relinquish center stage without leaving a more dignified impression. Thus, summoning a final bit of bluster, he attempts to establish a lasting truth about the world he has known:

> I learned three things in Zurich during the war. I wrote them down. Firstly, you're either a revolutionary or you're not, and if you're not you might as well be an artist as anything else. Secondly, if you can't be an artist, you might as well be a revolutionary. . . .
>   I forget the third thing. [Pp. 98–99]

In his own befuddled way Carr reinforces the major theme of the play: the difficult, uncertain roles of the artist and the revolutionary. Perhaps Carr's uncertainty represents our own uncertainty as to how we should establish meaning in our lives.

Every Good Boy Deserves Favour (1978)

Stoppard's growing concern with political matters reaches new intensity in *Every Good Boy Deserves Favour*, a short virtuoso play "for actors and orchestra." The primary setting is a cell which holds two men, both named Alexander Ivanov.

One, designated "Ivanov," is a genuine mental patient, whereas the other, designated "Alexander," is a political prisoner.
The opening scene establishes the essential dichotomy. Ivanov
plays the triangle in a mimed performance by an orchestra
that, though visible, is clearly in Ivanov's imagination. Eventually we hear the music, but the juxtaposition is created:
the irrational versus the rebellious; he who unconsciously
ignores the standards of society versus he who consciously
challenges those proprieties that he judges to be illegal and
immoral.

The scene switches quickly to a classroom where Alexander's
son, Sacha, is undergoing a manner of instruction, as geo-
metric truths are blended with moral didactics:

> SACHA: "A point has position but no dimenson."
> TEACHER: The asylum is for malcontents who don't know what
> they're doing.
> SACHA: "A line has length but no breadth."
> TEACHER: They know what they're doing, but they don't know
> it's antisocial.
> SACHA: "A straight line is the shortest distance between two
> points."
> TEACHER: They know its antisocial but they're fanatics.
> SACHA: "A circle is the path of a point moving equidistant to
> a given point."
> TEACHER: They're sick.
> SACHA: "A polygon is a plane area bounded by straight lines."
> TEACHER: And it's not a prison, it's a hospital.[27]

Here the second dichotomy is set, that between intellectual
truths and moral dicta, and their coindoctrination in a fascist
society. During this "education" the teacher reminds Sacha
that his father is being held at a mental hospital, and the boy
cries out "Papa." Immediately Alexander shouts his son's
name in return.

This predicament follows the theatrical pattern Stoppard
has cultivated. We are presented with an absurd world, or
rather two halves of an absurd world: the "hospital" and the

classroom. And we have a victim of that world: Alexander. But amid the bizarrely comic vision emerges a new element: an extraordinary compassion and anguish, of which the exchange of cries between father and son is but the initial instance.

The scene shifts back to the hospital, where Ivanov continues his mad charade. Suddenly from within the orchestra stands a violinist to assume the role of Doctor. Perhaps he can be understood first to tolerate Ivanov's fantasy, then to work to cure him. For a few moments the two banter about Ivanov's condition. Then Alexander speaks his own story, a horrific account laden with humor, but a horror nevertheless:

> They arrested a couple of writers, A and B, who had published some stories under different names. Under their own names they got five years and seven years hard labor. I thought this was most peculiar. My friend, C, demonstrated against the arrest of A and B. I told him he was crazy to do it, and they put him back into the mental hospital. . . .
>
> M compiled a book on the trials of C, I, J, K, and L, and with his colleagues N, O, P, Q, R, and S attended the trial of T who had written a book about his experiences in a labor camp, and who got a year in labor camp. [P. 16]

As always Stoppard presents an absurd world, confusing and terrifying, here concretized in the form of a Soviet regime,

The scene shifts to Sacha's classroom, and father and son exchange oral letters, which end with yet another outcry from Sacha. During this scene Stoppard offers a capsulized, comic-horror vision:

> ALEXANDER: Russia is a civilized country, very good at *Swan Lake* and space technology, and it is very confusing if people starve themselves to death. [P. 18]

In a sense this play is as openly passionate and full of rage as anything Stoppard has ever written, as he seems to be tossing aside that intellectual detachment so long intrinsic to his work. Such rage is manifest more fully in the vital exchange between Alexander and the Doctor. At first the reasoning seems a semblance of "Catch-22":

> DOCTOR: The idea that all people locked up in mental hospitals are sane while people walking about outside are all mad is merely a literary conceit, put about by the people who could be locked up. I assure you there's not much in it. Taken as a whole, the sane are out there and the sick are in here. For example, *you* are here because you have delusions that sane people are put in mental hospitals.
> ALEX: But I *am* in a mental hospital.
> DOCTOR: That's what I said. If you're not prepared to discuss your case rationally, we're going to go round in circles. [P. 25]

But when we learn that the Chief Doctor in charge of Alexander's case is actually a Doctor of Philology, it becomes apparent that the powers in charge are seeking to control Alex's language and thereby to control his thinking. As the Doctor says, "Your opinions are your symptoms. Your disease is dissent" (p. 31). And when Alexander threatens a hunger strike, the Doctor's kind demeanor vanishes, as he threatens. "If you don't eat something, I'll send for your son" (p. 31).

Eventually Sacha does arrive at the hospital, seeking his father, but he encounters instead Ivanov, whose ravings are a mad parody of Sacha's own "lessons":

> IVANOV: Everyone is equal to the triangle. That is the first axiom of Euclid, the Greek musician.
> SACHA: Yes, sir.
> IVANOV: The second axiom! It is easier for a sick man to play the triangle than for a camel to play the triangle. The third axiom! Even a camel can play the triangle! The pons asinorum of Euclid. Anyone can play the triangle no matter how sick. [P. 34]

The implication is unmistakable: nonsense and sense are equally meaningless when drilled into the passive minds of citizens and pupils.

Eventually Sacha shouts over another of his father's poetic recitations that Alexander should conform:

> SACHA: (*not singing*) Tell them lies. Tell them they've cured you. Tell them you're grateful.
> ALEX: How can that be right?
> SACHA: If they're wicked how can it be wrong?
> ALEX: It helps them to go on being wicked. It helps people to think they're not so wicked after all.
> SACHA: It doesn't matter. I want you to come home.
> ALEX: And what about all the other fathers? And mothers?
> SACHA: (*shouts*) It's wicked to let yourself die! [P. 36]

So Alexander relents in the presence of the Colonel, the Chief Doctor. Alexander does not protest his imprisonment and speak against injustice. Rather he offers identical answers to the same questions asked of the lunatic Ivanov. And then all four, Ivanov, Alexander, the Doctor, and the Colonel, join Ivanov's orchestra. Conforming madness reigns.

Has Alexander surrendered? To a certain extent the answer must be "yes," although his escape allows a comparatively happy ending. At least father and son both survive. They may have capitulated to the ruling order, but they have survived. And that survival is in itself an act of hope.

This play reaffirms some of Stoppard's fundamental theatrical precepts. Man is a victim of an absurd world, which he must try to understand and to which he must try to adjust. Oppression, cruel and unsympathetic, intrudes on his existence. Even the title itself, a mnemonic device which stands for the five notes on the line of the G-clef, suggests the programed, enforced conformity that constricts the citizens of the fascist state. Still, the play is filled with verbal fireworks, and the spectacle of the full orchestra on stage is a delightful conceit. A witty, yet tragic, one-act play, *Every*

Good Boy Deserves Favour is a reflection of Stoppard's ever more refined technique and sensibilities.

Professional Foul (1978)

Professor Anderson, the central figure of the television play *Professional Foul*, is reminiscent of Professor George Moore of *Jumpers*. Each is a philosopher, and each is confronted with conflicts and conundrums that demand commitment and resolution. But Anderson's world is not one of symbolic gymnasts, mad murderers, and bizarre detectives. Its absurdity takes the form of an intense evil in the face of which intellectual speculation can no longer exist in splendid detatchment.

Anderson's field is ethics, and as the play opens he is headed for Prague where, at a philosophical convention, he is to deliver a paper entitled "Ethical Fictions as Ethical Foundations." He arrives by plane and on the trip makes clear that his involvement in such issues is strictly academic. Indeed, his conversation with fellow philosopher McKendrick reveals Anderson's lack of awareness of his own profession. He is totally engrossed in private intellectual inquiry, and the intrusion of reality is never permitted.

That intrusion occurs, nevertheless, when Anderson is visited in his hotel room by Pavel Hollar, a native Czech and Anderson's former student in England. At first, Anderson is occupied with customary trivial amenities:

> ANDERSON: You got a decent degree, too, didn't you?
> HOLLAR: Yes, I got a first.
> ANDERSON: Of course you did. Well done, well done. Are you still in philosophy?
> HOLLAR: No, unfortunately.
> ANDERSON: Ah. What are you doing now?[28]

Finally the situation is established:

HOLLAR: I am a cleaner at the bus station.
ANDERSON: You wash buses?
HOLLAR: No, not buses—the lavatories, the floors where people walk and so on. [P. 57]

Hollar begins to speak of a doctoral thesis that he has written, the primary issue of which is "correct behavior," specifically as defined by the state. Anderson is intellectually intrigued:

> Quite. The difficulty arises when one asks oneself how the *individual* ethic can have any meaning by itself. Where does *that* come from? In what sense is it intelligible, for example, to say that a man has certain inherent, individual rights? It is much easier to understand how a community of individuals can decide to give each other certain rights. These rights may or may not include, for example, the right to publish something. In that situation, the individual ethic would flow from the collective ethic, just as the State says it does.
> *Pause*
> I only mean it is a question you would have to deal with.

But Hollar is not speaking in the abstract. He demands that Anderson take the manuscript out of the country for publication.

Thus Anderson's complacency is challenged. Are his intellectual speculations and ethical convictions mere academic exercise? Or are they purposeful considerations, applicable to "the real world?" In a sense Anderson's own life is at stake. Has it been strictly rhetorical foolishness? Or has it had some point?

The next day Anderson begins to investigate Hollar. When he visits Hollar's house, he learns that his former student has been arrested, and he finds himself under suspicion. Anderson is befuddled, uncertain how to proceed. He has never before encountered such a crisis, and his scholarly training seems of little help.

As counterpoint to Anderson's dilemma, the audience is presented with glimpses of philosophers debating issues, and in such scenes Stoppard's uniquely dexterous dialogue patterns sparkle:

> STONE: That's just the point, you see. When I say to you, "Tell me what you mean," you can only reply, "I would wish to say so and so." "Never mind what you wish to say," I reply. "Tell me what you *mean.*"
>
> FRENCHMAN: *Mais oui*, but if you ask me in French you must say, *"Qu'est-ce-que vous voudriez dire?"*—"What is that which you would wish to say?" *Naturellement*, it is in order for me to reply, *Je voudrais dire, etcetera.*"
>
> STONE (*excitedly*): But you are making *my* point—don't you see? [P. 94]

Amid the humorous banter, however, the ambitious young philosopher McKendrick delineates one personal theory, and he simultaneously and ironically hints at Anderson's own problem:

> The mistake that people make is, they think a moral principle is indefinitely extendable, that it holds good for any situation, a straight line crossing an endless two-dimensional graph of moral problem curves—they think that is what a principle *means*. [P. 97]

Such has always been Anderson's position, a position from which he has always surveyed the world safely. But McKendrick challenges that security:

> You can see that in three dimensions the line doubles back on itself. And what we call the catastrophe point is where the principle reverses itself, where a rational man would abandon it. [P. 97]

Anderson senses he has reached such a point, and he has no recourse but to take action.

Perhaps McKendrick's statements can be related to the two levels of absurdity that have so long dominated Stoppard's theatrical world. On the one hand, is the interior level, personal involvement with questions of identity and meaning. Then there exists the second layer, where all personal values must be adjusted to the circumstances that the world presents. Anderson is trapped between these levels, on the one hand debating philosophy, on the other struggling with his natural drives to help, his fears of being caught, and his desire to do "right" for himself, his former student, and freedom everywhere.

As further variation on this theme, Stoppard includes the drama of a football match taking place in Czechoslovakia during this story. Even this comparatively trivial event raises issues which echo Anderson's crisis. A player has committed an intentional foul to stop a goal, a "professional foul." He has deliberately broken the laws of the game. Was he justified? For his inquisition into this question, McKendrick is beaten up by a brutal footballer.

But Anderson resolves a more fundamental point. Delivering his paper at the colloquium, he departs from his prepared text, originally approved by the conference leaders. His topic is now "the conflict between the rights of individuals and the rights of the community" (p. 111).

This issue is virtually the same one pondered by George Moore. In *Jumpers* George seeks a universal truth, something permanent in a world of ever-changing values. Yet he has no involvements outside the intellectual world, and action is not demanded of him. Anderson, however, does have such conflicts, and his resolutions of the questions before him are similar to George's:

> In our time linguistic philosophy proposes that the notion of, say, justice, has no existence outside the ways in which we choose to employ the word, and indeed *consists* only of the ways we employ it. [P. 117]

Such is the judgment of Archie Jumper, whose values mirror A. J. Ayer's position. But Anderson does not stop there:

And yet common observation shows us that this view demands qualification. . . .There is a sense of right and wrong which precedes utterance. It is individually experienced and it concerns one person's dealings with another person. From this experience we have built a system of ethics which is the sum of individual acts of recognition of individual right. [Pp. 117–118]

Anderson has achieved a vision of right and wrong, which he applies to this situation:

If this is so, the implications are serious for a collective state or State ethic, which finds itself in conflict with individual rights, and seeks, in the name of the people, to impose its values on the very individuals who comprise the State. [P. 118]

As he continues fire alarms are set off. His ideas are not tolerated by the state which he attacks.

Anderson has arrived at a conclusion similar to the philosophy of George Moore. Anderson's, too, is based on an instinct of right and wrong and the conviction that within every human being lies that sense of objective right and wrong.

And Anderson does proceed to break the law. Knowing he will be searched at airport customs, he hides Hollar's thesis in McKendrick's satchel, and the manuscript goes through untouched.

More than any Stoppard protagonist, Anderson surmounts his world. He resolves personal questions, and he uses his solutions to encounter the buffetings of a brutal society that takes little pity on individual man. Surely the Czech government shares much with the Court of Elsinore, with the office where Gladys and Frank work, with the paint factory that employs Albert, and with the madness of World War I that surrounds Henry Carr. In *Professional Foul* rationality and morality triumph, if briefly. But it is triumph nonetheless.

Conclusion

Tom Stoppard's playwrighting career may be said to parallel the progress of twentieth-century theater. His first play, *Enter a Free Man*, is a realistic comedy-drama. He then moves into the world of absurdity, which is dramatized in *Rosencrantz and Guildenstern Are Dead*, in his fiction, and in several shorter plays. Yet at the same time, he extends the limits of absurdity by dramatizing the outside world concretely, as a part of a recognizable social system. And in his latest plays he creates characters who are not resigned to absurdity but are determined to battle against such a vision of the world—first through philosophical argument in *Jumpers*, and then through artistic and political revolution in *Artist Descending a Staircase*, *Travesties*, *Every Good Boy Deserves Favour*, and *Professional Foul*.

Stoppard's career as a playwright of ideas is particularly important at this time, when many contemporary avant-garde theater groups reject the concept of a playscript and consequently of a playwright. In addition, they have sought to tear down completely all distinctions between actor and audience, between art and life.

For instance, in the 1960s the Living Theater traveled worldwide performing "happenings" such as *Paradise Now*, *Frankenstein*, and *Dionysius in '69*. The primary goal of this group was to arouse such audience hostility that hidden aggressions would be released and thereby transformed into love. This variety of theatrical gestalt sprang from deep political convictions and from a devotion to anarchism. Thus a production like *Paradise Now* was conducted as an orgy of emotional and physical release, a desire to bring man back to his primitive, most natural self and to relieve him of the restraints of political oppression. For a few years the Living

Theater was an international sensation. However, in the early 1970s the movement disbanded, trapped by the dilemma of how to serve as a revolutionary force, to radicalize audiences, and yet still to survive commercially.[1]

A somewhat more stable company has been the Laboratory Theatre under the leadership of Jerzy Grotowski, who has created what he calls "the poor theatre." "Poor" in his sense means devoid of artifice, for artifice, even in art, is but another method of denying the pure human spirit:

> The theatre is not for him the synthesis of all arts. Costumes, settings, music, plays of light and text are accessory elements of a production, and the Laboratory Theatre has evolved in the direction of elimination, not eclectic synthesis. Grotowski is at the point today of extolling a poor theatre, in direct opposition to a total theatre which throws itself on all the new resources of sound and light with that devouring hunger characteristic of our technically obsessed and gadget-crazy time.[2]

At the core of Grotowski's art is the actor—one who must spend years in exacting training, learning to extend the uses of one's voice and body and, in fact, to surrender one's entire personality and way of life to the concept of disciplined total performance.

Grotowski eschews dramatic literature as integral to theater:

> Even the text is for him no longer anything more than one of the elements of production—he calls it 'the springboard and the challenge.' The theatre does not have as its mission or *raison d'être* the illustration of the text, but the creation of a particular response to it; the dramatic text is a question to be answered. Grotowski rejects what Flaszen calls the 'philological' theatre, one with pretentions—or intentions—that are literary, philosophical, or polemical.[3]

He and his company seek selected passages they feel are appropriate to their style and present these in production. Among the most notable of Grotowski's creations, many of which take years to formulate and are forever undergoing revision, are *Akropolis* (1962) and *The Constant Prince* (1965).

Given such extraordinary theatrical events as these companies and others like them offer, the Theater of the Absurd seems almost tame. The private, subtle loneliness of Beckett's desolate landscapes and the unspoken hells that Pinter's characters suffer, these have little in common theatrically with the chaos of the Living Theater or the poetic exertions of Grotowski's productions. These companies see aesthetic fulfillment in the unhampered release of hostility and energy, the reduction of the human being to animalistic primitivism. At least in the Theater of the Absurd, which also depicts the pathetic plight of man, the playwright's consciousness and creativity afford man the right to regard himself as more than a beast.

But surely it is possible for an artist to present man with a greater measure of dignity. In most of Tom Stoppard's plays his characters are struggling, not surrendering. They are aware of absurdity, yet they are unwilling to resign themselves to it. Earlier I wrote of the excruciating consciousness of man caught in the absurdist dilemma. Man understands the nature of his world, yet he dares not give in. He must seek to bring meaning to what he strongly suspects is a meaningless existence. In Stoppard's latest plays his protagonists have sought specific channels through which to pursue meaning and to find significance for themselves. They seek faith in rationality. They seek faith in human emotions. They seek faith in relationships with other people. The seek faith in their humanity. Their battles are not necessarily successful. But the very struggle brings a dignity to life and aids in that drive to reach beyond absurdity.

Tom Stoppard is still a comparatively young man, but his nineteen pieces considered here comprise a substantial body of creative work. Of course, one must recognize that an analysis of a man's writing in the middle of his career can but assume the character of a progress report. Still, it can be seen that Stoppard has clearly emerged from one theatrical idiom and that his latest plays may well signal the emergence of another.

The idiom which has had the greatest impact on Stoppard's writing is "the absurd," a movement which shattered traditions of staging, character, dialogue, and plot. Theatrical order can never be the same.

But Stoppard has not been content to leave man in the absurdist void. True, his works always have elements of absurdity, manifested generally in his protagonists, who are nonentities swept into the action of a world they cannot understand. And Stoppard almost always displays their predicaments comically. However, he also develops undertones of seriousness, emphasizing the need for some action other than surrender to counteract absurdity. He explores man coping with the artistic world in such plays as *Rosencrantz and Guildenstern Are Dead, Artist Descending a Staircase, The Real Inspector Hound,* and *Travesties.* He explores man coping with political systems in *If You're Glad I'll be Frank, Travesties,* and *Every Good Boy Deserves Favour.* He explores man coping in society in such plays as *Enter a Free Man, Albert's Bridge, Where Are They Now,* and *Professional Foul.* He explores man and his faith, both religious and secular, in such plays as *Jumpers* and *Travesties.* Of course, in none of these works does any single theme long dominate, and the four areas are usually interlocked.

If one may single out any unifying element in Stoppard's works, it is his faith in man's mind. He rejects the irrational, the reliance on emotion instead of intellect, the retreat from independent thought. And this commitment is the foundation for his theatrical techniques.

First, he makes free use of form: linear movement, flashbacks, plots within plots, and innumerable references to other literary works. Yet amid all the clutter and episodic action, a structure emerges, a tribute to the organizing powers of the playwright's rationality and his expectations of the audience's ability to grasp that structure.

Second, his emphasis on variety of language, in terms of

brisk pace, literary allusions, and double and triple meanings, reaffirms his own belief in man's ability to communicate. He manages at the same time to make his language amusing, yet richly woven with ideas.

Third, he maintains a concern for people, demonstrated more than ever in his latest plays. Even though his characters may be isolated, lost figures, they are never turned into the one-dimensional figures of standard absurd drama. Always Stoppard insists on their dealing with ideas, questions, and their own responsibilities as human beings. Ultimately, his plays may be understood as an affirmation of man's humanity in the face of all obstacles.

In all likelihood, Tom Stoppard will continue to break new dramatic ground. This book will, I hope, serve as an introduction to what has already proven to be a highly significant playwrighting career, one that marks the beginning of the post-absurdist movement.

Notes

Introduction

1. William Barrett, *Time of Need* (New York: Harper and Row, 1972), p. 353.
2. Frederick A. Pottle, *The Idiom of Poetry* (Ithaca, N.Y.: Cornell University Press, 1941), p. 21.
3. Clive Barnes, "A London Trio," *New York Times*, 9 August 1972, p. 49.
4. Jack Richardson, "Theatre," *Commentary* 57 (June 1974): 79–80.
5. By 1960 Samuel Beckett's plays *Waiting for Godot* (1952), *Endgame* (1957), and *Krapp's Last Tape* (1958) had been produced to great acclaim, as had most of Ionesco's major works, including *The Bald Soprano* (1950), *The Lesson* (1951), *The Chairs* (1952), and *Rhinoceros* (1959). Genet had completed *The Balcony* (1956) and *The Blacks* (1958). In addition, Harold Pinter had begun his career with such works as *The Room* (1957), *The Birthday Party* (1958), and *The Caretaker* (1960). In 1961 Martin Esslin's *The Theatre of the Absurd* was published, the first extensive treatment of these playwrights and others such as Adamov, Albee, and Simpson as part of a disparate, yet still very important, literary and dramatic movement.
6. "Something to Declare," *Sunday Times* (London), 25 February 1968, p. 47.

Chapter 1

1. Martin Esslin, *The Theatre of the Absurd*, rev. ed. (Garden City, N.Y.: Doubleday, 1968).
2. John Killinger, *World in Collapse: The Vision of Absurd Drama* (New York: Dell, 1972).
3. Thomas Bishop, *Pirandello and The French Theater* (New York: New York University Press, 1960), p. 123.
4. Esslin, *Theatre of the Absurd*, pp. 6–7.
5. William Barrett, *Time of Need*, (New York: Harper and Row, 1972), p. 105.
6. Arnold P. Hinchliffe, *The Absurd*, The Critical Idiom, no. 5 (London: Methuen, 1969), p. 81.

Chapter 2

1. Much of the biographical information was obtained from the following sources: "Playwright–Novelist," *New Yorker*, 4 May 1968, pp. 40–41; Giles Gordon, "Interview with Tom Stoppard," *Transatlantic Review* 29 (Summer 1968): 17–25; and Mark Amory, "The Joke's the Thing," *Sunday Times Magazine* (London), 9 June 1974, pp. 65–75.

2. "Waiting for Hamlet," *New Republic*, 27 April 1972, p. 26.

3. "Playwright-Novelist," p. 40.

4. Amory, "The Joke's the Thing, p. 69.

5. "The Angry Young Men" was a nickname attached to a group of English writers who came to prominence in the 1950s. Generally of working- or middle-class origins, they expressed the disillusion of a generation that was educated at the universities but was yet unable to break into the restricted power circles of British politics and education. Their works are characterized by a disgust with upper-class snobbism, materialism, and hypocrisy. Among the most notable playwrights were John Osborne (*Look Back in Anger*, 1956), Arnold Wesker (*The Kitchen*, 1962), and John Arden (*Sergeant Musgrave's Dance*, 1959). Among the leading fiction writers were Alan Sillitoe (*The Loneliness of the Long Distance Runner*, 1959) and Kingsley Amis (*Lucky Jim*, 1954). The tradition has been kept alive in the theater by David Storey (*The Contractor*, 1970, and *The Changing Room*, 1972).

6. "From 'Rosencrantz' to Our Time," *New York Times*, 7 April 1968, Section 2, p. 8.

7. "At the Start," *New Yorker*, 6 January 1975, p. 50.

8. Amory, "The Joke's the Thing," p. 69.

9. Arthur Miller, *Death of a Salesman* (New York: Viking Press, 1949), p. 33.

10. Robert Bolt, *Flowering Cherry* (London: William Heinemann, 1958), p. 16.

11. Ibid.

12. Tom Stoppard, *Enter a Free Man* (New York: Grove Press, 1968), p. 10. All quotations in the text are from this edition.

13. "Snake Oil," *Newsweek*, 31 August 1970, p. 77.

14. Mollie Panter-Downes, review of *Rosencrantz and Guildenstern Are Dead*, *New Yorker*, 6 May 1967, pp. 179–80.

15. Clive Barnes, review of *Rosencrantz and Guildenstern Are Dead*, *New York Times*, 17 October 1967, p. 53.

16. "Waiting for Hamlet," p. 148.

17. "Absurdism Altered: *Rosencrantz and Guildenstern Are Dead*," *Drama Survey* 7 nos. 1 and 2 (Winter 1968–69): 52–53.

18. "The Road to Dusty Death," *Plays and Players* 14, no. 9 (June 1967): 12–15.

19. *Rosencrantz and Guildenstern Are Dead* (New York: Grove Press, 1967), p. 14. All quotations in the text are from this edition.

20. "Theatre Chronicle," *Hudson Review* 20, no. 4, (Winter 1967): 665.

21. "To Be and Not to Be," *Reporter*, 16 November 1967, pp. 39–40.

22. "Who's on First?" *Commonweal*, 10 November 1967, p. 172.

23. Richard Gilman, *The Making of Modern Drama* (New York: Farrar, Straus and Giroux, 1974), p. 179.

24. All quotations from Shakespeare are from *Shakespeare: Complete Plays and Poems*, ed. Neilson and Hill (Boston: Houghton Mifflin, 1942).

25. Luigi Pirandello, *Naked Masks*, ed. Eric Bentley (New York: E. P. Dutton, 1952), p. 276.

Chapter 3

1. Jill Levenson, "Views From a Revolving Door: Tom Stoppard's Canon to Date," *Queen's Quarterly* 78, no. 3 (Fall 1971): 439.
2. Tom Stoppard, *Lord Malquist and Mr. Moon* (1966; rpt. London: Faber and Faber, 1974), p. 192. All quotations in the text are from this edition.
3. Levenson, "Views from a Revolving Door," p. 441.
4. Tom Stoppard, "Reunion;" "Life, Times: Fragments;" "The Story;" in *Introduction 2: Stories by New Writers* (London: Faber and Faber, 1964), p. 122. All quotations in the text are from this edition.
5. Samuel Beckett, quoted in Martin Esslin, *The Theatre of the Absurd*, rev. ed. (Garden City, N.Y.: Doubleday, 1968), p. 32.

Chapter 4

1. Stoppard's unpublished plays include two stage plays, "The Gamblers" (1965) and "Dogg's Our Pet" (1971); a radio play, "M is for Moon among Other Things" (1964); and several television plays, including "Teeth" (1967), "Another Moon Called Earth" (1967), "Neutral Ground" (1968), and "The Engagement" (1970). The last was also a screenplay and, in an earlier version, a radio play entitled "The Dissolution of Dominic Boot" (1964).
2. Tom Stoppard, *Albert's Bridge* and *If You're Glad I'll Be Frank*, (London: Faber and Faber, 1969), p. 41. All quotations in the text are from this edition.
3. Samuel Beckett, *Proust* (1931; rpt. New York: Grove Press, n.d.), p. 2.
4. Richard Coe, *Samuel Beckett* (New York: Grove Press, 1964), p. 17.
5. Beckett, *Proust*, p. 4.
6. Jill Levenson, "Views from a Revolving Door: Tom Stoppard's Canon to Date," *Queen's Quarterly* 78, no. 3 (Fall 1971): 433.
7. Tom Stoppard, *A Separate Peace* in *Playbill Two*, ed. Alan Durband (London: Hutchinson Educational Ltd., 1969), p. 108. All quotations in the text are from this edition.
8. Tom Stoppard, *Albert's Bridge* and *If You're Glad I'll Be Frank*, (London: Faber and Faber, 1969), p. 9. All quotations in the text are from this edition.
9. *The Myth of Sisyphus and other pieces*, trans. J. O'Brien (New York: Vintage Books, 1959), p. 91.
10. Levenson, "Views from a Revolving Door," p. 434.
11. A. E. Housman, *The Collected Poems of A. E. Housman* (New York: Holt, Rinehart and Winston, 1965), p. 111.
12. Levenson, "Views from a Revolving Door," p. 434.
13. Tom Stoppard, *The Real Inspector Hound* (New York: Grove Press, 1968), p. 9. All quotations in the text are from this edition.
14. "A Grin without a Cat," *Times* (London) 22 June 1968, p. 19.
15. Tom Stoppard, *Dirty Linen and New-Found-Land*, (New York: Grove Press, 1971), p. 21. All quotations in the text are from this edition.
16. Nahma Sandrow, *Surrealism: Theater, Arts, Ideas* (New York: Harper and Row, 1972), p. 21.

17. Anna Balakian, *Surrealism: The Road to the Absolute*, rev. ed. (New York: E. P. Dutton, 1970), pp. 204–5.

18. Tom Stoppard, *After Magritte* (London: Faber and Faber, 1971), p. 17. All quotations in the text are from this edition.

19. Tom Stoppard, *Artist Descending a Staircase* and *Where Are They Now* (London: Faber and Faber, 1973), p. 66. All quotations in the text are from this edition.

Chapter 5

1. Kathleen Halton, "Tom Stoppard," *Vogue*, 15 October 1967, p. 112.

2. Tom Stoppard, *Jumpers* (New York: Grove Press, 1972), pp. 74–75. All quotations in the text are from this edition.

3. "Love Among the Logical Positivists," *Sunday Times* (London), 9 April 1972, p. 16.

4. Ibid.

5. Ibid.

6. G. E. Moore, *Principia Ethica* (1903; rpt. Cambridge: At the University Press, 1960), p. 17.

7. A. J. Ayer, *Language, Truth, and Logic* (1936; rpt. New York: Dover, 1946), p. 107.

8. Ayer, *Love Among the Logical Positivists*, p. 16.

9. Wesley C. Salmon, ed., *Zeno's Paradoxes* (New York: Bobbs-Merrill, 1970), pp. 8–9.

10. Ibid, pp. 10–11.

11. Ayer, *Love Among the Logical Positivists*, p. 16.

12. Samuel Beckett, quoted in Martin Esslin, *The Theatre of the Absurd*, rev. ed. (Garden City, N.Y.: Doubleday, 1968), p. 32. See also Luke 23: 43.

13. Review of *Jumpers*, Nation, 18 May 1974, p. 637.

14. *Artist Descending a Staircase* and *Where Are They Now?* (London: Faber and Faber, 1973), p. 15. All quotations in the text are from this edition.

15. Esslin, *Theatre of the Absurd*, p. 317.

16. "The Zealots of Zurich," *Times Literary Supplement* (London), 12 July 1974, p. 744.

17. Tom Stoppard, *Travesties* (London: Faber and Faber, 1975), p. 18. All quotations in the text are from this edition.

18. Richard Ellmann, *James Joyce* (New York: Oxford University Press, 1959).

19. James Joyce, *Ulysses* (New York: Modern Library, 1934), p. 573.

20. Ibid, p. 587.

21. Oscar Wilde, *Five Plays* (New York: Bantam, 1961), p. 227.

22. "Ambushes for the Audience: Towards a High Comedy of Ideas," *Theatre Quarterly* 4, no. 14 (May-June 1974): 13.

23. Ibid, pp. 12–13.

24. Wilde, *Five Plays*, p. 215.

25. Ibid, p. 236.

26. Samuel Beckett, *Three Novels* (New York: Grove Press, 1965), p. 414.

162 / Beyond Absurdity

27. Tom Stoppard, *Every Good Boy Deserves Favour* and *Professional Foul* (New York: Grove Press, 1978), pp. 15–16. All quotations in the text are from this edition.
28. Ibid, p. 57.

Conclusion

1. Margaret Croyden, *Lunatics, Lovers and Poets* (New York: Dell, 1974), p. 131.
2. Raymonde Temkine, *Grotowski* (New York: Avon, 1972), p. 63.
3. Ibid.

Bibliography

Plays by Tom Stoppard

Stoppard, Tom. *After Magritte*. London: Faber and Faber, 1971.

_____. *Albert's Bridge* and *If You're Glad I'll Be Frank*. London: Faber and Faber, 1969.

_____. *Artist Descending a Staircase* and *Where Are They Now?* London: Faber and Faber, 1973.

_____. *Dirty Linen* and *New-Found-Land*. New York: Grove Press, 1976.

_____. *Enter a Free Man*. New York: Grove Press, 1972.

_____. *Every Good Boy Deserves Favour* and *Professional Foul*, New York: Grove Press, 1978.

_____. *Jumpers*. New York: Grove Press, 1971.

_____. *The Real Inspector Hound*. New York: Grove Press, 1969.

_____. *Rosencrantz and Guildenstern Are Dead*. New York: Grove Press, 1967.

_____. *A Separate Peace* in *Playbill Two*. Edited by Alan Durband. London: Hutchinson Educational Ltd., 1969.

_____. *Travesties*. London: Faber and Faber, 1975.

Other Writings by Tom Stoppard

Stoppard, Tom. "A Case of Vice Triumphant" (review of *Venice Preserv'd*). *Plays and Players* 14, no. 6 (March 1967): 16–17.

_____. "I'm Not Keen on Experiments." *New York Times*, 8 March 1970, section II, p. 17.

_____. "Just Impossible" (review of *The Impossible Years*). *Plays and Players* 14, no. 4 (January 1967): 28–29.

_____. *Lord Malquist and Mr. Moon*. 1966; reprint ed., London: Faber and Faber, 1974.

_____. "Playwrights and Professors." *Times Literary Supplement*, 13 October 1973, p. 1219.

————. "The Positive Maybe." *Author* 78 (Spring 1967): 17–19.

————. Review of *Orghast* by Ted Hughes. *Times Literary Supplement*, 1 October 1971, p. 1174.

————. Review of *A Supplement to the Oxford English Dictionary*, *Punch*, 12 December 1972, pp. 893–894.

————. "Something to Declare." *Sunday Times*, 25 February 1968, p. 47.

————. "Reunion"; "Life, Times: Fragments"; "The Story" in *Introduction 2: Stories by New Writers*. London: Faber and Faber, 1964.

————. "Yes, We Have No Banana." *The Guardian*, 10 December 1971, p. 10.

Selected Criticism

"Ambushes for the Audience: Towards a High Comedy of Ideas" (interview with Tom Stoppard). *Theater Quarterly* 4, no. 14 (May-June 1974): 3–17.

Amory, Mark. "The Joke's the Thing." *Sunday Times Magazine* (London), 9 June 1974, pp. 65–75.

Asmus, Walter D. "*Rosencrantz and Guildenstern Are Dead*." *Shakespeare Jahrbuch* 106 (1970): 118–31.

Ayer, A. J. "Love Among the Logical Positivists." *Sunday Times* (London), 9 April 1972, p. 16.

Babula, William. "The Play-Life Metaphor in Shakepeare and Stoppard." *Modern Drama* 15 (December 1972): 279–81.

Baumgart, Wolfgang. "Hamlet's Excellent Good Friends: Beobachtungen zu Shakespeare und Stoppard." In *Englische Dichter der Moderne: Ihr Leben und Werk*. Edited by Rudolf Sühnel and Dieter Riesner. Berlin: Schmidt, 1971, pp. 588–98.

Bennett, Jonathan. "Philosophy and Mr. Stoppard." *Philosophy* 50, no. 191 (January 1975): 5–18.

Berlin, Normand. "*Rosencrantz and Guildenstern Are Dead*: Theater of Criticism." *Modern Drama* 16 (December 1973): 269–77.

Bigsby, C. W. E. *Tom Stoppard*. Writers and their Work. Essex: Longman Group Ltd., 1976.

Brustein, Robert. "Waiting for Hamlet." *New Republic*, 4 November 1967, pp. 25–26.

Callen, Anthony. "Stoppard's Godot: Some French Influences on Post-War English Drama." *New Theatre Magazine* 10, no. 1 (Winter 1969): 22–30.

Carroll, Peter. "They Have Their Entrances and Their Exits: *Rosencrantz and Guildenstern Are Dead*." *Teaching of English* 20 (1971): 50–60.

Cook, B. "Tom Stoppard, the Man behind the Plays." *Saturday Review*, 8 January 1977, pp. 52–53.

Ellman, Richard. "The Zealots of Zurich." *Times Literary Supplement* (London), 12 July 1974, p. 744.

Farish, Gillian. "Into the Looking-Glass Bowl: An Instant of Grateful Terror." *University of Windsor Review* 10, no. 2 (1975): 14–29.

Gale, John. "Writing's My 43rd Priority." *Observer*, 17 December 1967, p. 4.

Giankaris, C. J. "Absurdism Altered: *Rosencrantz and Guildenstern Are Dead*." *Drama Survey* 7, nos. 1 and 2 (Winter 1968–69): 52–58.

Gitzen, Julian. "Tom Stoppard: Chaos in Perspective." *Southern Humanities Review* 10 (1976): 143–52.

Goldstein, Leonard. "A Note on Tom Stoppard's *After Magritte*." *Zeitschrift für Anglistik und Amerikanistik* 23 (1975): 16–21.

Gordon, Giles. "Interview with Tom Stoppard." *Transatlantic Review* 29 (Summer 1968): 17–25.

Gussow, Mel. "Stoppard Refutes Himself, Endlessly." *New York Times*, 26 April 1974, p. 36.

Halton, Kathleen. "Tom Stoppard." *Vogue*, 15 October 1967, p. 112.

Harper, Keith. "The Devious Road to Waterloo." *Guardian*, 7 April 1967, p. 7.

Harris, Wendell V. "Stoppard's *After Magritte*." *Explicator* 34 (1976), item 40.

Hayman, Ronald. *Tom Stoppard*. London: Heineman, 1977.

James, Clive. "Count Zero Splits the Infinitive: Tom Stoppard's Plays." *Encounter*, November 1975, pp. 68–71.

Kennedy, Andrew K. "Old and New in London Now." *Modern Drama* 11 (February 1969): 437–46.

Keyssar-Franke, Helen. "The Strategy of *Rosencrantz and Guildenstern Are Dead*." *Educational Theatre Journal* 27 (1975): 85–97.

Lee, R. H. "The Circle and Its Tangent." *Theoria* 33: 37–43.

Leech, Michael. "The Translators." *Plays and Players* 20, no. 7 (April 1973): 36–37.

Leonard, Virginia E. "Tom Stoppard's *Jumpers*: The Separation from Reality." *Bulletin of the West Virginia Association of College English Teachers* 2, no. 1 (1975): 45–56.

Levenson, Jill. "Views from a Revolving Door: Stoppard's Canon to Date." *Queen's Quarterly* 78, no. 3 (Fall 1971): 431–42.

Mansat, A. "R & G sont morts." *Les Langues Modernes* 64, no. 4 (July 1970): 396–400.

Nakanishi, Masako. "Tom Stoppard no Sekai-kyoto to Genjitsu no Mondai." *Oberon* 34 (1971): 53–71.

Norman, Barry. "Tom Stoppard and the Contentment of Insecurity." *Times* (London), 11 November 1972, p. 11.

Pasquier, Marie-Claire. "Shakespeare ou le lien common: A propos de *Rosencrantz and Guildenstern Are Dead* de Tom Stoppard." *Recherches Anglaises et Américaines*, no. 5 (1974), pp. 110–120.

Prideaux, Tom. "Uncertainty Makes the Big Times." *Life*, 9 February 1968, pp. 72–76.

Quinn, James E. "Rosencrantz and Guildenstern Are Alive and Well in the Classroom." *Missouri English Bulletin*, 26 October 1970, pp. 16–19.

Schwartzman, Myron. "Wilde about Joyce?: Da! But My Art Belongs to Dada!" *James Joyce Quarterly* 13 (1975): 122–23.

Taylor, John Russell. "Tom Stoppard—Structure + Intellect." *Plays and Players* 17, no. 10 (July 1970): 16–18.

"Tom Stoppard: Theatre Checklist." *Theatrefacts* 2 (May–July 1974): 2–9.

Tynan, Kenneth. "Tom Stoppard." *New Yorker*, 19 December 1977, pp. 41–46.

Watts, Janet. "Interview with Tom Stoppard." *Guardian*, 21 March 1973, p. 10.

Wetzsteon, Ross. "Tom Stoppard Eats Steak Tartare with Chocolate Sauce." *Village Voice*, 10 November 1975, p. 121.

Zeh, Dieter. "Tom Stoppard: *Rosencrantz and Guildenstern Are Dead*" in *Das Zeitgenossische Englische Drama: Einführung, Interpretation, Dokumentation*. Frankfurt: Athenäum, 1975, pp. 229–46.

Index